RAIL AROUND BIRMINGHAM

THE BLACK COUNTRY AND SOUTH STAFFORDSHIRE

▲ Rail freight around Birmingham: 7F 0-8-0 No 49021 thunders through Brettell Lane station with a coal working bound for Stourbridge Power Station in the mid-1960s. *Brian Moone, courtesy of Kidderminster Railway Museum*

▼ Forty years later a Class 66 EWS loco heads a ballast train on Railtrack duty loading in the ballast sidings at the south end of Bescot yard, viewed from the southern end of the Walsall platform. *Author, 10 June 2004*

Rail Around Birmingham

THE BLACK COUNTRY AND SOUTH STAFFORDSHIRE

Andrew Doherty

·RAILWAY HERITAGE·
from
The NOSTALGIA Collection

First published in 2009

British Library Cataloguing in Publication Data

A catalogue record for this book is available from the British Library.

ISBN 978 1 85794 322 1

Silver Link Publishing Ltd
The Trundle
Ringstead Road
Great Addington
Kettering
Northants NN14 4BW

Tel/Fax: 01536 330588
email: sales@nostalgiacollection.com
Website: www.nostalgiacollection.com

Printed and bound in the Czech Republic

Acknowledgements

There are many people who have helped immeasurably with the research and preparation of this book to whom I owe a great debt of gratitude. Whether sourcing photographs and information, or reading drafts and providing sounding-boards for my ideas, to everyone who has aided me in the writing of this book I offer my sincere thanks.

In particular I'd like to thank David Johnson, Frank Jennings, Lawrence Hogg, Peter Hackney, Audie Baker at Kidderminster Railway Museum, Paul Baxter, Simon Dewey, Ray Durrant, Bernard Shaw, Dave Williams, John Edgington, Michael Hale and Michael Whitehouse for photographs, and Will Adams and all at Silver Link Publishing for having faith in this project.

For help over and above the call of duty my special thanks go to Dave Bathurst, Roger Shenton, Mark Norton, Paul Walker and Roger Carpenter.

Finally, I'd like to thank my wife Vicky and son Christopher, who have had to put up with more than their fair share of railway-related outings and endless outbursts of 'There used to be a station there' and 'I'm just going to stop the car to look at that' when out and about; to them both I say thanks for both your love and support.

Contents

Preface   6

Introduction   7

Route 1   Stourbridge Junction to Dunstall Park   11

Route 2   The Wombourn Branch   32

Route 3   Stourbridge Junction to Oldbury Town   44

Route 4   Hunnington to Dudley   53

Route 5   Sandwell & Dudley to Wolverhampton
             High Level and the Princes End Branch   60

Route 6   Swan Village to Wolverhampton Low Level
             and Dudley   72

Route 7   Dudley to Lichfield City and the Darlaston Loop   80

Route 8   Wylde Green to Lichfield Trent Valley   94

Route 9   Tame Bridge Parkway to Wednesfield Heath   102

Route 10   Sutton Town to Wolverhampton High Level   110

Chasewater Railway   125

Index of locations   128

Preface

As a child I spent many happy hours sitting in the café at Dudley Zoo gazing out of the windows, much to my mother's annoyance, watching the comings and goings at the Dudley Freightliner Terminal that stood on the site once occupied by the joint LMS/GWR Dudley station. These regular school holiday outings were my introduction to the railways of the Black Country, and to the Black Country itself, an area that has since become a fascination for me not only for its rich railway heritage but also for its now sadly demised industrial history.

This focus of this volume in the 'Rail Around Birmingham' series moves beyond the County Borough of Birmingham boundaries to the lines in the surrounding areas collectively known as the 'Black Country' and those of South Staffordshire. While the definition of what constitutes the Black Country is open to interpretation, for this purposes of this book I am referring in the main to the passenger lines between Dudley, Sandwell, Walsall, Wolverhampton, Halesowen and Stourbridge and incorporating the northern end of what is now the Cross City Line, through Sutton Coldfield and Lichfield in South Staffordshire.

The aim of this book, therefore, is to provide a record of the region's railway heritage, to provide a complete map of the Black Country and South Staffordshire passenger railway network routes to Birmingham and between the aforementioned towns and cities from its inception to the present day, listing all the passenger stations, past and present, with both contemporary and historical photographs, line maps and OS coordinates for those readers who wish to explore the sites themselves.

I hope that this book will be as big an eye-opener to readers who don't remember the region in its heyday as researching it was for me, in showing what a rich railway history has existed in the area, and what of that history is still left to explore and enjoy. However, as a caveat to that statement, with the speed of redevelopment in the area I would urge readers to explore what is left of the railways of the Black Country sooner rather than later, and I hope that, as you will see through this book, you will not be disappointed!

Introduction

For geological reasons, the Black Country provided the perfect setting for the Industrial Revolution, sitting, as it did, on the vast South Staffordshire 'thirty foot' coal seam. When industrialisation began to sweep the nation, due to the outcropping of the seam in parts of the region, both open cast and drift mining could take place, providing the fuel for rapid industrial growth. The demand for coal to feed the boom in heavy industry drove the exploration of deeper mining techniques, with collieries developing throughout the area that necessitated rapid improvements in the transport infrastructure.

This need was initially supplied by the building of a network of canals that criss-crossed the region ferrying coal from colliery to factory, and raw materials and finished goods both locally and throughout the country. As the unrivalled transport system, canal companies, and privately owned navigations, profited significantly from the industrial growth in the region. However, in the early part of the 19th century another form of transportation was developing in the industrial north of England that was proving the ideal means of transporting goods and materials at higher speeds than the canals, and with significantly greater benefits.

The growth and potential financial rewards to be found in the Black Country were not lost on the emerging railway companies and the race was on to connect the region to the embryonic railway networks gradually extending their reach throughout the country. Indeed, privately owned 'tramways' were already in use in the region, largely for the transportation of coal in and around collieries and to canal wharves, but no network existed between them as such. The situation was to change dramatically on 4 July 1837 with the coming of the Grand Junction Railway (GJR). This was constructed from Warrington through a new Wolverhampton station at Wednesfield Heath and on to a temporary station at Vauxhall in Birmingham, before completion of a new station at Curzon Street, which was adjacent to that proposed by the London & Birmingham Railway (LBR). This would, in effect, provide a unified route from the docks at Liverpool, through the industrial Midlands and to London.

This move marked the beginning of the railway boom in the Black Country, with a myriad of other railway companies racing to secure their slice of the market. The major players to establish firm footholds in the region were the London & North Western Railway (LNWR), formed by an 1846 merger between the GJR, LBR and Manchester & Birmingham Railway, the Midland Railway (MR), and the Great Western Railway (GWR).

With the opening of Bescot Bridge station on the Grand Junction Railway in 1847 – billed as the first station to serve Walsall, albeit some 2 miles away – soon to be followed by a more central Walsall station under the Midland Railway – the LNWR and Oxford, Worcester & Wolverhampton Railway (OWWR) opening at Dudley, and the LNWR and GWR reaching Wolverhampton by the mid-1850s, the railways of the region were taking shape. In addition to the major players, a plethora of 'independent' railway companies – who were by and large heavily tied to, and in many cases soon to be incorporated by, the 'big three' were busy providing numerous link lines and branches.

The GWR in particular aggressively sought to monopolise the riches of the area with a stringent policy of absorbing many of the independent railways. For example, the Oxford, Worcester & Wolverhampton Railway, under guidance from the GWR, ran its line from Worcester and up through Stourbridge to Dudley, only to fall foul of the GWR with its move to enter Wolverhampton High Level in conjunction with the LNWR, a move that was blocked. The OWWR later formed part of the West Midland Railway, finally becoming part of the GWR. The ill-fated Birmingham, Wolverhampton & Dudley Railway began work on its line from Birmingham Snow

Hill to Wolverhampton and was soon be absorbed by the GWR. Such manoeuvres led to the GWR's dominance in the east of the region, with the LNWR and the MR largely sharing the spoils elsewhere.

With the railway 'Grouping' in 1923, the Black Country's railways were amalgamated into the GWR and the London, Midland & Scottish Railway (LMS), the latter absorbing both the LNWR and MR lines as well as a share of those still independent of the 'big three'. While profits were certainly being made, dark clouds were on the horizon for the railway companies. The increasing emergence of road transport – buses, trams, cars and trucks – was beginning to erode both passenger and goods revenue. Furthermore,

the coalfield that had provided the spur and fuel for the industrial boom was beginning to show signs of exhaustion in certain areas, leading to a string of colliery closures. The GWR, in acknowledgement of a potentially harmful shift in traffic, mooted ill-fated ventures in turning what were goods-only, and largely mineral, lines into passenger concerns, such as the branch through Wombourn (the GWR spelling of Wombourne), which did little to ignite the interest of potential passengers with the result that services were withdrawn after just seven years. The LMS, which had followed a similar process some years earlier with its Brownhills branch, also conceded defeat and withdrew passenger services in 1930, the line reverting to goods and colliery traffic.

◀ An impressive structure on the Halesowen Railway – 660 feet long and 100 feet high – was Dowery Dell trestle viaduct near Hunnington, removed upon closure of the line in 1964. *13 January 1958; Roger Shenton*

◀ After lying dormant for many years, Wolverhampton Low Level station is being redeveloped into a shopping and entertainment complex. Here clearance work is well under way. *7 September 2006*

While there was additional small-scale shrinkage in the network, the temporary nationalisation of the railways for the duration of the Second World War saw them put into overdrive – operating as they did through the industrial heart of the war machine – with little time for repair. This resulted in the network becoming somewhat of a spent force by the end of the conflict. However, a political sea-change by 1948 saw the most radical shake-up to hit the railways since their inception with the complete network being purchased by the Government as a national industry. British Railways was born.

As with other regions, nationalisation spelled the beginning of the 'rationalisation' of the railways. Competition between railway companies had given rise to multiple stations in many areas, and while some had fallen by the wayside earlier in the century as the result of amalgamation and the Grouping, there were still a significant number of, in some instances, relatively small villages and suburbs served by two stations. Greet Bridge, Tipton and Princes End were examples, with Wolverhampton being the largest example in the Black Country.

The monumental investment required to bring the railways back to their peak, coupled with diminishing returns due to the increasing dominance of road traffic, brought about the realisation in government that all was not well with the railways and that economic viability and prudence would have to be applied; a process of rationalisation had therefore begun by the late 1950s. However, this process gathered pace with 1963's *The Reshaping of British Railways* – or the 'Beeching Report' as it became known after the then British Railways Chairman Dr Richard Beeching. This was the result of an extensive study of the network, and proposed that a third of the country's total railway mileage should be closed and that numerous passenger lines be retained for goods traffic only in an attempt to streamline the system and retain only those parts where potential revenue would balance favourably against expenditure.

The Report was to impact on the Black Country particularly heavily, with many of its lines to close

completely. Dudley, for example, would lose its passenger rail connection altogether and the majority of branch lines would be closed, thus removing much of the GWR's legacy in the region. This was further compounded by the decision to electrify the Stour Valley line from New Street to Wolverhampton High Level, which rang the death knell for Wolverhampton Low Level, as the line from Snow Hill was to be closed and lifted in 1972, the line from Stourbridge having already been closed in 1962.

The once flourishing colliery and industrial traffic couldn't save the region's railways as this too had dwindled, with the majority of collieries closing and the near complete dominance of road haulage taking away the main revenue stream that had inspired the early railway companies to invest in the area in the first instance. Even the conversion of the Dudley site to a rail freight concentration depot under the flagship 'Freightliner' project floundered and was eventually abandoned by 1989.

Such was the extent of the decimation of the region's railways that the renaissance experienced in Birmingham with such success – the Cross City Line, for example – was not economically viable in the Black Country due to the eagerness with which lines had been lifted during the 1960s and '70s. While there have been some successes, such as the reopening of the Walsall-Hednesford line, the era following the privatisation of the railways in 1994-96 has done little to reinvigorate the region's railway scene, and the immense geographical changes experienced in the area have by and large negated the possibility of ever reopening many of the closed lines. Apart from the Midland Metro light rail route opening in 1999 along the ex-GWR Snow Hill to Wolverhampton line, little has changed. Extensions to the Metro system are frequently proposed but fail to materialise and other grandiose projects, such as the reopening of Wolverhampton Low Level station and even the Wombourn branch, have come to nothing.

It would appear, sadly, that the zeal with which the railways were systematically dismantled in the region has proved to be irreversible.

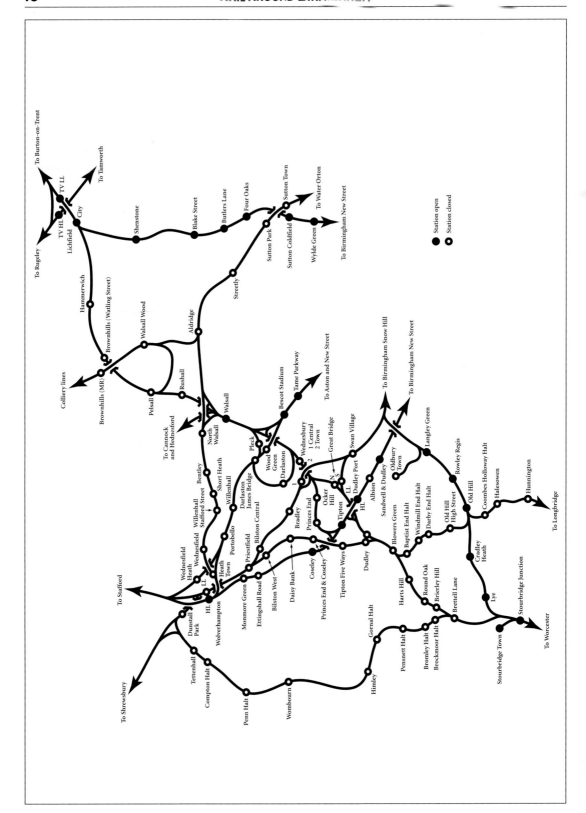

Route 1:
Stourbridge Junction
to Dunstall Park

With the exception of Stourbridge Junction and Stourbridge Town, the first route we traverse is now sadly bereft of stations, and in part, the rails themselves have been lifted and sites redeveloped altogether. Predominantly, the route follows the Oxford, Worcester & Wolverhampton Railway's Stourbridge to Wolverhampton Low Level line – soon to come under the auspices of the GWR – and takes in the 'Town Extension', a short branch through Stourbridge Town station originally terminating at Stourbridge Basin transhipment facility.

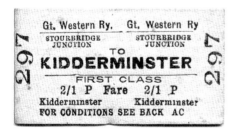

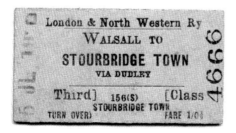

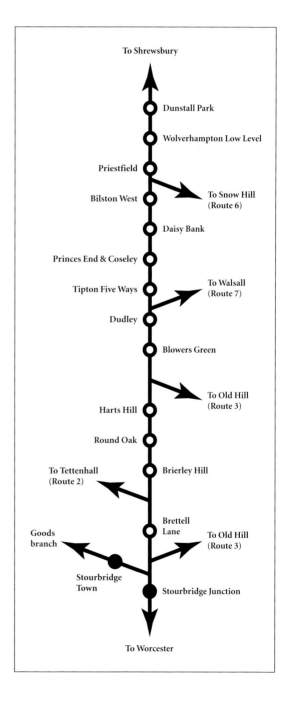

Stourbridge Junction　Grid reference 390960/283290

The original Stourbridge station lay just to the north of the present station (off what is now Junction Road, a few minutes' walk from the present station) and opened in 1852 under the Oxford, Worcester & Wolverhampton Railway. The station and the junction (which came into being when the GWR opened the branch to Stourbridge Town in 1879) were moved by the GWR to its present location. Much of this station has changed over the years, particularly during the late 1970s and 1980s, but it still retains character – no mean feat when you consider some of the other stations in a similar position in the region!

◀ The booking hall/entrance to the station is not the original from 1901, as can be discerned, but was built in 1988/89 following demolition of the much larger, two-storey original. *13 February 2004*

◀ The roofing canopies at the station replaced the typical GWR dart-fringed originals during the late 1970s, but the current design has retained some character for the original platform buildings. This photograph of the station from the ends of Platforms 1 and 2 is looking towards Birmingham, and gives a good view of the roofing, which, although of a modern flavour, is not totally out of keeping. One of the significant changes that can be discerned here is that the station originally consisted of two island platforms, but has now lost Platform 4 to the current car park (extreme right). *13 February 2004*

◀ From the end of platforms 1 and 2 we see the remaining signal box in situ as No 150104 passes, beyond which are sidings that used to be the goods yard, still extant but no longer for goods purposes. The branch to Stourbridge Town is off-camera to the left; the line seen in the left of the shot, passing the signal box, is a spur off the branch. *13 February 2004*

Stourbridge Town

Grid reference 390415/284175

One of the more endearing stations of the region, Stourbridge Town was originally opened in 1879 and closed in 1915, reopening in 1919. The ex-GWR station now sits on a single-line branch from Stourbridge Junction, which terminates here.

▲ The view from Parkfield Road bridge gives a good perspective of the station site. Although the old station was demolished in 1978, the iron latticework footbridge survived, but was rendered pointless with the proposed new design for the single-track station and was dismantled during the 1980s, together with the bridge carrying the line over what is now Stourbridge bus station. *13 June 2004*

▶ This is the buffer-stop and booking office at Stourbridge Town looking towards Stourbridge Junction. The station building itself is not in its original position – originally it lay on the opposite side of the track. The line here originally continued to a transhipment wharf at Stourbridge Basin, and was double track. *23 July 2003*

Brettell Lane

Grid reference 390810/286265

The station opened in 1852 under the Oxford, Worcester & Wolverhampton Railway and is the final station south of Dudley to remain closed, as just south of this station the line joins with the GWR Stourbridge Extension on which all stations remain open today. Brettell Lane closed in 1962 together with the others on this stretch of track. Although the trackbed remains, it is not in use for passenger services but provides a goods link, including that to the nearby Moor Street yard.

◀ This is where the station building used to be, looking towards the Brettell Lane overbridge, which has undergone considerable concrete remodelling since the photograph on page 2 was taken. The photographer is standing roughly where the empty mineral wagons were in that photograph, with the site of the booking office immediately to the rear. *23 October 2003*

▼ We are now looking down what remains of one of the entrances to the station from Brettell Lane – there are a couple of runs of blue brick and various other clues that give away its prior function. The walkway now leads to a small car park that is roughly on the site of the old station building. The area ahead is now occupied by the Breener Industrial Estate, but once housed various station outbuildings and the goods yard. *23 October 2003*

▶ Immediately beyond Brettell Lane lies the bridge carrying Bull Street over the tracks, and through it we can just make out the sidings entering Moor Street yard. The line splits ahead, the Dudley route curving to the right and, to the left, the line running into the EWS yard and forming the beginning of the Wombourne branch (see Route 2). Buffer stops can also be discerned on the old wagon sidings that once occupied this spot. *23 October 2003*

Brierley Hill

Grid reference 391472/287387

The station opened in 1858 on the Oxford, Worcester & Wolverhampton Railway between Round Oak and Brettell Lane and in its latter years took on a rather ramshackle appearance.

Interestingly for a station in this area, it had no goods facilities other than a single siding to serve a nearby factory. The station closed to passengers on 30 July 1962 and was demolished in 1968.

▼ Viewed from the footbridge shortly prior to closure, we are looking south with Bradleymore Road running alongside the line to the left of the shot. From 1962 until demolition the station was retained to deal with parcels traffic. *16 June 1962; G. E. S. Parker, courtesy of Kidderminster Railway Museum*

◀ Unfortunately it is not possible to get a good shot to compare with the 1962 photograph at Brierley Hill today. However, here we are roughly adjacent to the footbridge site, but this time looking towards Round Oak with Bradleymore Road to the right. As can be seen, nothing remains of the station at track level today. *23 October 2003*

Round Oak

Grid reference 391935/287852

Round Oak station was opened by the Oxford, Worcester & Wolverhampton Railway in 1852 and succumbed to closure, together with the other stations (apart from Harts Hill, which had closed in 1916) on the Dudley-Stourbridge Junction line, in 1962. This was the third station south of Dudley and was later to come under the auspices of the GWR following its absorption of the successor to the OWWR, the West Midland Railway, in 1863.

▼ Doomed to close, Round Oak Station is seen here in 1962. The landscape of the surrounding area has changed considerably since the time of the station: Round Oak Steel Works closed in 1980 and the site now houses the Merry Hill Shopping Centre/Waterfront development, which occupies a vast tract of land to the right of the signal box in this view. It is surprising that Round Oak station, or a new site nearby, has not been utilised for a passenger service to Merry Hill. *G. E. S. Parker, courtesy of Kidderminster Railway Museum*

▲ Looking back from the A461 bridge, we are looking directly down to the spot where once the platforms were situated, the Dudley platform to the right and the Stourbridge platform to the left, showing that clearance work was total. *23 October 2003*

▼ We are now on the A461 Dudley Road looking across to the entrance to the Dudley platform – the gap in the wall to the right of the shot. Interestingly, a notice post can also be discerned to the left of the gateway. The building on the extreme right is the Blue Brick public house, which can also just be discerned in the extreme left of the 1962 picture. *23 October 2003*

Harts Hill

Grid reference 392897/288538

One of the region's forgotten stations, Harts Hill opened on the ex-OWWR line under GWR ownership in 1895. The end of the 19th century saw investment by the GWR in the perceived lucrative area of the Black Country that eventually failed to materialise in terms of passenger numbers. Harts Hill was opened under that misjudged optimism on a line opened in 1852 just

a short distance from Blowers Green, itself a late-comer to the line in 1862, and the junction with the 'Bumble Hole line' opened in 1878. Harts Hill, however, fared far worse than those of the 'Bumble Hole line' and only kept itself open to passengers for 21 years, closing during the First World War in 1916, never to reopen.

▲ Despite its closure in 1916, a 1960s *A to Z* shows the station position and marks it as a hollow 'dot', indicating it is still a functioning site but not for passengers. From this we can surmise that the site lived on for goods purposes until the mid-1960s (it had disappeared from maps by 1970). Unfortunately, the station failed to ignite the interest of railway historians (or photographers), who only seemed to acknowledge it in passing, if at all. Here we are looking down at the station site from Highgate Road. *19 November 2004*

◄ Walking through the Highgate Road entrance yielded this view of the remnants of track-lifting with pieces of removed track now strewn over the trackbed as the route heads off towards Blowers Green. *19 November 2004*

Blowers Green

Grid reference 394352/289555

The opening of the station as Dudley Southside & Netherton in 1878 coincided with the opening of the 'Bumble Hole line' to Old Hill, which branched off the Dudley line a couple of hundred yards south of this station. The station became Blowers Green in 1921 and remained such until closure in 1962, although trains from Dudley to Old Hill continued to pass through the site until 1964.

▶ Seen from the entrance to the Dudley platform from New Road one month before closure, BR Standard Class 2 2-6-0 No 78008 pauses at the station with a Stourbridge to Wolverhampton working before entering the tunnel leading Dudley station. *16 June 1962; G. E. S. Parker, courtesy of Kidderminster Railway Museum*

▼ As close as can be reproduced, this view also shows the station site and the tunnel from New Road looking towards Dudley, with the ticket office immediately to the left, off-camera. The embankment to the right has been increased in height with the building of the Dudley Bypass since the station's operational days. *23 October 2003*

▼ The booking hall still stands on New Road, although all traces of other buildings have disappeared. Considering it is now 41 years since closure it is in excellent condition and worth a look – even its entry canopy is intact! It is possible to get round to the back of the building, but the stairwell connecting it to the platform level has long since been removed and the rear of the building therefore has a narrow ledge at the edge of a steep drop to trackbed level. *23 October 2003*

Dudley

Grid reference 395525/290650

Dudley station opened in 1860 and was at the intersection of routes of the Oxford, Worcester & Wolverhampton Railway and the South Staffordshire Railway, later incorporated into the GWR and LNWR/LMS respectively. The station has significant goods facilities and was open for passengers until 1964; in 1967 work began to clear the site in readiness for its conversion to a Freightliner depot, a function that it served until 1989 when the site was finally abandoned, with the lines on which it stood closing to all through traffic in 1993. However, the constant debate over an additional Midland Metro light rail line to the Merry Hill shopping complex has been enough to ensure that at least some vestige of railway remains at the site, although whether or not this will ever come to fruition is a moot point.

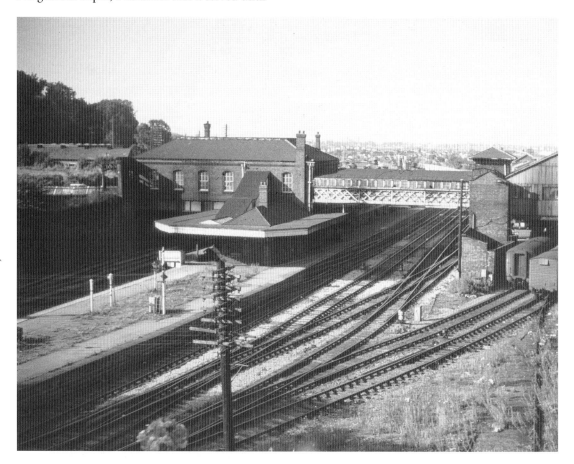

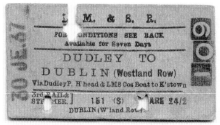

▲ In the mid-1960s Dudley station is in limbo, with passenger services having ceased and the forthcoming conversion to a Freightliner terminal – which would involve the total demolition of the station buildings seen here – yet to commence. At this time the station site was largely relegated to rolling-stock storage prior to work beginning on site clearance. The ex-GWR station is seen here to the left, with the ex-LMS station to the right. *23 September 1966; David Bathurst*

▲ Following final closure the site has almost totally been reclaimed by nature, as we see in this reverse view taken from roughly the site of the canopy on the GWR station in the 1966 photograph. The only lines remaining at the site today are 'mothballed' and are seen here heading off towards Blowers Green and, to the rear of the photographer, Dudley Low Level. *15 July 2003*

▼ The remaining rails are seen here curving away towards Dudley Port Low Level. To the left is the site of the Freightliner terminal, now just an overgrown field. *15 July 2003*

Tipton Five Ways

Grid reference 394745/292282

Like Princes End, for example, Tipton station suffered either from lack of foresight or from railway company rivalry to be the dominant station in a particular area; it was opened by the Oxford, Worcester & Wolverhampton Railway in 1853 as Tipton, just one year after the LNWR had

also opened a Tipton station a short distance away. It wasn't until 1950 that this station had 'Five Ways' added to its nameboard and 'Owen Street' tagged on to the ex-LNWR facility – surely just renaming one of the stations would have avoided any confusion!

▲ Looking towards Wolverhampton not long before closure, the station has a run-down appearance with dilapidated fencing and unkempt and crumbling platform surfaces. Immediately beyond the Wolverhampton platform, the parapet of the bridge carrying the line over Sedgley Road West can just be discerned. *16 March 1962; P. J. Garland collection*

▼ Today nothing remains of the station site as a new development of houses (Oxford Way) has been built on the spot and the embankment leading to the station site's

convergence with ground level at the junction of Poplar Road and Menin Road has been removed. The station stood immediately to the left of the photograph – however, if you look to the bottom of the road you can still see the remains of the bridge that once carried the line over Sedgley Road West. *15 December 2003*

▼ Sedgley Road West bridge remains are the only (so far as can be discerned) visible signs of the railway at this location. *15 December 2003*

Princes End & Coseley   Grid reference 395175/293703

This station was opened in 1853 by the Oxford, Worcester & Wolverhampton Railway on that company's Wolverhampton Low Level to Dudley line. It was one of two stations to serve the small area of Princes End: the LNWR also opened a station in 1863 just a few minutes' walk from here. Interestingly, the station originally opened as Princes End; '& Coseley' was not added until 1936, which must have been somewhat confusing.

▲ A year after closure, this is the station looking towards Tipton Five Ways. It has a rather 'temporary' feel, with its wooden platforms and waiting rooms. Note also the ticket office perched precariously on the side of the embankment. *16 March 1963; P. J. Garland collection*

▼ Taken from the same spot on Bradleys Lane, the station site, now encroached on by new housing beyond the shrubbery, is a wasteland. *24 October 2003*

▼ The view from Bradleys Lane towards Daisy Bank and Wolverhampton, with the station site to the rear, shows a parkway and walk now following the trackbed, but it would appear that the trackbed has been raised and/or the road level lowered since the line closed. *4 October 2003*

Daisy Bank

Grid reference 394972/295090

The station opened in 1854 and closed, as did many, for the period of the Great War, 1916-19, finally closing in 1962 with the withdrawal of passenger services along the Dudley to Wolverhampton Low Level route.

▲ As can be seen, the station had a somewhat rural GWR feel to it, although located in the heart of the industrial Midlands. In this view, taken during its final operational year and looking towards Wolverhampton, the distinctive GWR darted valancing and latticework footbridge can be seen. The entrance to the Wolverhampton platform from Rounds Road can be seen to the left. *16 June 1962; G. E. S. Parker, courtesy of Kidderminster Railway Museum*

◀ The trackbed is now a 'nature walk' – which I would suggest somewhat cynically is a synonym for it not being of significant saleable value, so has been left to pasture. The photographer is standing roughly at the spot once occupied by the platforms, looking towards Bilston West with Lane Street bridge in the distance. *5 December 2003*

Bilston West

Grid reference 394520/295887

The station was opened by the Oxford, Worcester & Wolverhampton Railway in 1854 as just Bilston ('West' added in 1950). It later came under GWR control (although the extent to which the OWWR was autonomous from the GWR is debatable).

▲ Here we see the station immediately prior to closure, looking somewhat dilapidated. I believe this view is looking towards Wolverhampton, but having only ever seen one previous photograph of the site, and with its total reclamation since, I cannot confirm this with any degree of certainty. *16 June 1962; G. E. S. Parker, courtesy of Kidderminster Railway Museum*

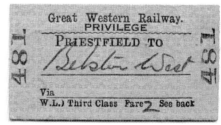

▶ Unfortunately, with the realignment of the road and the closure of the railway more than 45 years ago, nothing remains today to indicate the station site. As a rough guide, the station stood to the left of the car ahead on an embankment, accessed by a flight of steps next to what was then a bridge over the road. However, while remnants of the embankment do still exist off-camera to the right, for discernible signs of the railway here you need to go half a mile or so in either direction from this spot to pick up the trail. *5 December 2003*

◄ Heading towards Wolverhampton for half a mile or so brings you to Millfields Road, which still retains its bridge over the now defunct trackbed. Bilston West is to the right and Wolverhampton to the left. *5 December 2003*

Priestfield

Grid reference 393545/296975

Priestfield opened in 1854 at the junction of the Oxford, Worcester & Wolverhampton Railway's line from Stourbridge Junction and the GWR's line from Snow Hill to Wolverhampton Low Level. The station closed in two stages due to the fact that it served two routes: the line to Stourbridge Junction via Dudley closed in 1962 with complete closure for the station in 1972 following the closure of the line from Snow Hill to Wolverhampton Low Level.

▼ Viewed from the entrance pathway down from George Road, this view shows the Stourbridge line to the right and the line to Snow Hill curving away to the left. With the loss of main-line services in 1967 the station soon fell into complete disrepair, being only served by a single-car diesel unit shuttle service between Wolverhampton Low Level and Snow Hill. Final lifting of the line took place shortly after total closure in 1972. *16 March 1963; P. J. Garland collection*

▲ A recent similar perspective shows that the site is once again rail-connected between Snow Hill and Wolverhampton in the form of the Midland Metro light rail service, which has a 'Priestfield' Metro stop the other side of the bridge from which the photograph was taken and occupying the site of the former goods sidings. The notable absentee here is the line to Stourbridge Junction, which would have continued straight ahead just past the second set of overhead supports, but is now filled in. *5 December 2003*

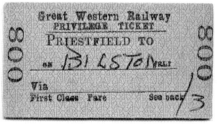

▶ The view from Ward Street, on what was the bridge over the Stourbridge Junction line looking along what remains of the trackbed towards Bilston West, clearly indicates the path of the former line but is now a 'linear park' and walkway. *5 December 2003*

Wolverhampton Low Level

Grid reference 392060/298920

Wolverhampton Low Level station was opened in 1854 by the Oxford, Worcester & Wolverhampton Railway, later to fall under the auspices of the GWR. Unlike its High Level neighbour, it was closed to passengers in 1972, but continued to function as a parcels depot until 1981.

▲ In this view from the autumn of 1969 we get a rare glimpse of the goods facilities at the site during demolition – the passenger station is to the right of the photograph. Although the lines have been lifted and the goods depots are being removed, the lines were soon back in business as the passenger station site was converted for use as a parcel distribution depot. *Peter Hackney*

◀ On a snowy January day in 1979, diesel shunter No 08782 is in use as depot pilot. Seen from the bridge carrying Sun Street over the lines, the footbridge is still in situ although the goods sheds being demolished in the earlier photograph are no more, having once stood to the right of the shot. *Simon Dewey*

▲ In 2003 the station makes a forlorn scene in the heart of Wolverhampton as a derelict and overgrown ruin. This view is taken again from Sun Street but the bridge over the track has now been removed, thus truncating the line for good at the southern end of the site. *3 September 2003*

▼ Three years later the station site is in the throes of a major redevelopment as the Station Plaza retail and entertainment complex. The station forecourt has changed little since its operational days and the buildings seen here are all original and have weathered the test of time remarkably well! *7 September 2006*

▲ Again viewed from Sun Street, we see that much clearance has taken place at Wolverhampton Low Level as part of the Station Plaza shop/bar complex. Although the northbound platform and station buildings appear to have been preserved, the rest of the site is apparently being dismantled and bulldozed. *7 September 2006*

Dunstall Park

Grid reference 391357/300305

Dunstall Park station had seemed to be an alluring prospect for a visit for some time, due in no small part to its close proximity to the former GWR Stafford Road loco works, which can be seen in the photograph below. Unfortunately, the station, which opened in 1896 and enjoyed considerable passenger traffic for the nearby racecourse, closed in 1968, and although the line is still in use and receives regular traffic, the site is now cleared with just a few signs as to its former visible upon close inspection.

▼ Ex-GWR 'Hall' Class 4-6-0 No 6933 *Birtles Hall* runs an engineers' train tender-first through Dunstall Park, with the passenger platforms ahead and, in the left distance, the looming structure of the former GWR Stafford Road locomotive works. *5 March 1961; J. Wood, courtesy of Kidderminster Railway Museum*

▲ A similar recent perspective, looking towards Shrewsbury, shows that nothing appears to remain at track level to indicate the former station's existence. Furthermore, the Stafford Road works has long since closed, together with the racecourse – such is the pace of change in the region! *13 November 2006; Paul Baxter*

▶ However, upon entering the Wulfrun Trading Estate, which now stands on the site of Stafford Road works, the part-filled remains of the subway that enabled passengers to move between platforms could still be seen. While then in good repair, it can be seen that the floor level has been considerably raised since its operational days. *7 September 2006*

Route 2:
The Wombourn branch

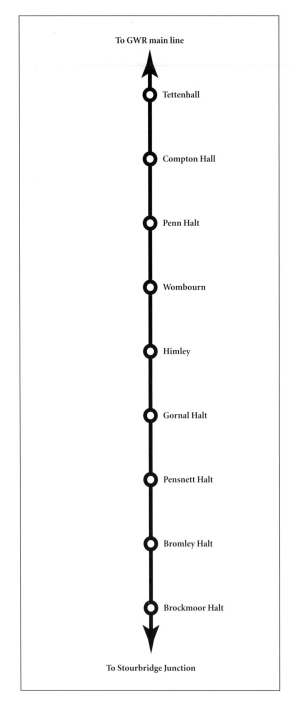

To GWR main line

Tettenhall

Compton Hall

Penn Halt

Wombourn

Himley

Gornal Halt

Pensnett Halt

Bromley Halt

Brockmoor Halt

To Stourbridge Junction

A late-comer to the region's railway scene, the Wombourn branch – misspelled minus the 'e' in an attempt by the GWR to avoid confusion with Wimborne (LSWR) – the line served as a prime example of Great Western folly. Frequently described as a 'stillborn' passenger route, the 12-mile line opened in 1925 serving largely rural and sparsely populated areas between the outskirts of Dudley and Wolverhampton. It did little to ignite the enthusiasm of the few people who lived close to its stations and halts, a fact exacerbated by the fact that it went largely from small hamlet to small hamlet, so even the growing number of commuters wouldn't have availed themselves of its services. The line closed to passengers in 1932, but proved a useful route for bypassing Wolverhampton and was retained for goods traffic until 1965, when it was closed and soon lifted. Much of the trackbed remains today, together with various structures, as a footpath between Himley and Tettenhall, and with the track still in situ between Brockmoor and Pensnett. Only the section between Pensnett and Himley is largely untraceable today.

Brockmoor Halt

Grid reference 391033/287085

Brockmoor Halt was the first stop heading north from the junction with the GWR Stourbridge to Wolverhampton via Dudley line, and was not seen even by the GWR as a passenger prospect of any real significance, thus even denied 'platform' status. Interestingly, a milepost was provided at the station informing passengers that the distance to Paddington was 144¾ miles!

▲ 0-6-0PT No 7705 pulls a goods working through Brockmoor Halt towards Brettell Lane after passing under Moor Street bridge. The station had closed to passengers in 1932, some 23 years earlier, but both platforms are still in situ. *12 April 1955; Michel Hale*

▼ Here we are looking down at the site of the halt from Moor Street, with Moor Lane yard and the old Dudley line just out of sight around the right-hand bend ahead. To the left can be discerned the access pathway sloping down from the road to the southbound platform. *4 February 2004*

▼ This shot was taken between the platforms looking north through Moor Street bridge. The Stourbridge platform remains at the site, buried beneath brambles and undergrowth to the right; the northbound platform has long since been removed. *4 February 2004*

Bromley Halt

Grid reference 390573/288063

Bromley Halt opened with the line in 1925 as an unstaffed halt, and remained in use until the cessation of passenger services some seven short years later.

▲ 'Modified Hall' Class 4-6-0 No 7915 *Mere Hall* passes through the long-disused Bromley Halt, about to pass under Bromley Lane bridge. Of note is the GWR 'Pagoda' shelter on the northbound platform and the overgrown and disused Stourbridge Extension Canal to the left of the photograph. *10 March 1961; Brian Moone, courtesy of Kidderminster Railway Museum*

▼ A similar more recent perspective reveals that the Stourbridge Extension Canal has vanished, having been drained and filled in to the height of the roadway and now occupied by the back gardens of a recent housing development to the left. The Stourbridge line, however, is still in situ and the remains of the Stourbridge platform can just be discerned on the right. *4 February 2004*

▼ Following a rather perilous route down from the road bridge along what was once the entrance pathway to the Stourbridge platform, but now a knife-edged ledge, we have arrived at track level with the Bromley Lane bridge to the rear, looking from the end of the Stourbridge platform towards Wombourn. Both platforms are completely intact albeit heavily overgrown and strewn with rubbish dumped over the back garden fences of houses that now border the cutting on both sides. *4 February 2004*

Pensnett Halt

Pensnett Halt's short life as a passenger facility only spanned seven years but the sidings beyond the halt site fared considerably better, providing an adjacent distribution centre for Perrier bottled water, among other items, during its operational years. Both the line and the sidings are still in situ at the site and EWS recently proposed a much-opposed reopening of the line here to a new distribution terminal to be built a short distance away.

▲ Looking towards Gornal and the bridge carrying High Street, we see the long-abandoned Pensnett Halt with its platforms still in situ, the decrepit signal box and lower-quadrant signal. *16 June 1962; G. E. S. Parker, courtesy of Kidderminster Railway Museum*

▼ Looking down from High Street, the trackbed is now a walkway. The signal box stood to the right roughly adjacent to the building seen at the top of the photograph. *4 February 2004*

▼ The multiple sidings are seen from High Street, with the former Perrier distribution centre located where the lorries can be seen to the left. A ground-frame now sits beside the track – off-camera – which replaced the signal box in later years. *4 February 2004*

Gornal Halt

Grid reference 390452/290115

A handful of sites in the region – Bilston West and Windmill End spring to mind – gave me the most headaches in pinpointing their exact location. Gornal Halt was another! Due to the complete remodelling of the surrounding area, there are no clues as to its existence today and the line, which is highly traceable throughout its route elsewhere, disappears completely at Gornal.

▲ The halt is seen here some 30 years after closure to passenger traffic. The line ran roughly diagonally between Stallings Lane, from where the photograph was taken, and Tansey Green Lane, the bridge for which can be seen ahead. As with Bromley Halt, GWR 'Pagoda' platform shelters long outlived the passenger service at the halt: note the posts for the station nameboard to the left. *16 June 1962; G. E. S. Parker, courtesy of Kidderminster Railway Museum*

◀ Here we are in roughly the spot from where the 1962 photograph was taken and, as can be seen, the cutting has been filled in. To complicate matters further, the alignment of both Stallings Lane and Tansey Green Lane – ahead on the right – have been altered since the days of the line, making precise identification of the location nigh on impossible. *19 November 2004*

Himley

Grid reference 387545/291040

The majority of stops on the GWR's Wombourn branch were merely halts, but Himley was deemed worthy of station status serving, as it did, one of the more highly populated areas on the route.

Unfortunately, the GWR overestimated the demand for a railway service and the station closed with the line in 1932.

▲ Following withdrawal of goods services along the line in 1965, the removal of the track commenced in 1967 and, as can be seen here, the station buildings had been demolished and the line reduced to single-track some time previously. *9 July 1967; Dave Bathurst*

▼ The trackbed is now utilised as the South Staffordshire Railway Walk. The route is pleasantly rural and runs through land previously owned by the Earl of Dudley and on part of which Baggeridge Colliery once stood, a mine

that was once served by the single-track predecessor to the Wombourn branch. The northbound platform is still extant to the left and the station buildings would have been just ahead; beyond them the bridge took the lines over Himley Lane. *4 February 2004*

▼ What is now a picnic area was once the point of entry to the station and was occupied by the main station building, of which nothing remains today. *4 February 2004*

Wombourn

Grid reference 387020/293885

The station from which the branch took its name was originally known as The Bratch – the name of a watercourse running near the site – but this was quickly dropped in favour of a more geographical name. When compared with the other stops on the line, Wombourn was a station of some size with a water tower on the northbound platform and a signal box. However, the relative grandeur of the station did nothing to stimulate passenger growth and the station closed to passengers in 1932.

▲ Some 32 years after the cessation of its brief role as a passenger station, it appears to have been well maintained and is still intact as a group of enthusiasts inspect the site. *13 June 1964; P. J. Garland collection*

◄ The preserved Wombourn station stands beside the South Staffordshire Railway Walk, in this view looking towards Stourbridge. *4 February 2004*

▲ The Stourbridge platform building, the main station building and booking office, is still in situ and now used as a tea room for ramblers. *4 February 2004*

▶ This fascinating structure is the weighbridge office, as Wombourn had a goods yard and several sidings, and is in perfect, if unused, condition. Unfortunately, the weighbridge is no longer at the site, but there remain a significant number of railway relics to make the site worthy of a visit! *4 February 2004*

Penn Halt

Grid reference 386310/296210

A location of little significance on the Wombourn branch, Penn Halt was opened in 1925 by the GWR in anticipation of good passenger patronage that never materialised. A brief tour of the surrounding relatively rural area largely answers the question as to why passenger numbers were never high. This point was not completely missed by the GWR, which provided just a single-platform halt, this section of the line being single-track.

▲ Greyhound Lane and a signpost at the site now inform us that the line forms the South Staffordshire Railway Walk. There appears to be nothing left at the site to show its past; the only structure was a single platform, which, unusually for station/halt sites on this line, appears to have been removed. *4 February 2004*

◄ At the site of the platform, we are now looking towards Stourbridge through Greyhound Lane bridge, the only structure hinting at the site's past. *4 February 2004*

Compton Halt

Grid reference 388312/298740

Compton Halt, a stone's throw from Tettenhall station, consisted of a single platform perched high on an embankment and, as with the rest of the line, suffered from dismal passenger receipts. While Wombourn and Tettenhall stations were of significant size for the establishment of goods facilities, which extended their futures beyond the withdrawal of passenger services in 1932, Compton Halt was not.

▶ This is the entrance to the halt from Bridgnorth Road. This section of the line forms part of a 'nature trail/walk' with the signpost on the left of the entrance reading 'Welcome to Smestow Valley Local Nature Reserve'. *4 February 2004*

▼ Here we see the halt looking towards Wombourn. The platform has been preserved, and appears in near perfect condition. The line was single-track, so this platform served both up and down trains. *4 February 2004*

Tettenhall

Grid reference 389170/299915

Surviving for goods traffic until 1965, when the last train passed over the line on 24 June, Tettenhall station was a large concern with goods shed and sidings, the former still standing today.

These features helped the station live on beyond the cessation of passenger services in 1932, but couldn't help it escape the complete closure of the line in 1965.

▲ In this view looking north, with the line closed and work on lifting the track and dismantling the facilities in progress, the down platform building cuts a sorry figure. *27 December 1967; David Bathurst*

◄ The down platform waiting room has been preserved, with the goods shed visible on the right.. Unfortunately, the now necessary staircase built into the side of the platform and the safety rail outside the waiting room spoil what would otherwise be a view of the station directly comparable with it in its heyday. The protruding sign on the building, in keeping with the station architecture, reads 'Valley Park – Tettenhall Station'; the building is now used as a Park Ranger station. *19 November 2004*

▲ The station booking office still stands in Meadow View – previously known as Station Road. I was aware that the trackbed and down platform waiting room had survived but was pleasantly surprised to see that the booking hall and the weighbridge building (the small brick hut nearest to the camera) had survived and seemed in a reasonable state of repair. *19 November 2004*

▼ This is the goods shed still displaying 'Goods Depot' on its wall and appearing in very good repair. Although looking remarkably 'period', there are now large roller-shutters at either end, which either obscure the original archway entrances to the shed or have necessitated the archways' removal – it was impossible to tell without gaining access to the interior. Since closure, the building has been used as a workshop and, in later years, as the storage site for the local mobile library. *19 November 2004*

Route 3: Stourbridge Junction to Oldbury Town

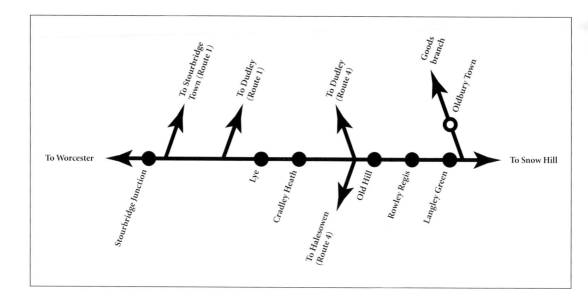

The second route we traverse from Stourbridge Junction follows the GWR route to Birmingham New Street, which, unlike Routes 1 and 2, is still in use today providing for commuter traffic from Worcester and up through the Southern Black Country approaches to Birmingham. Opening from Stourbridge to Old Hill in 1863 under the Stourbridge Railway, the line was extended by the GWR in 1867. It has suffered some losses during its history but enjoys a flourishing rail service currently operated by London Midland.

Stourbridge Junction – see Route 1, page 12

Lye

Grid reference 392185/284655

Sitting on the latter-day GWR's Stourbridge Extension, Lye station opened in 1863 under the short-lived, and short-routed, Stourbridge Railway, and has the odd distinction of being the station with the shortest name in Britain!

▶ Lye station is viewed from the car park, with a general air of disrepair about the site. The rather shabby station building and meagre facilities do little to reflect the original buildings at the site and its now closed significant goods facilities. *23 July 2003*

▶ This view is looking down at the station from Dudley Road in the direction of Birmingham as a Class 150 DMU departs for Snow Hill. Since my earlier visit the station has received a 'makeover', with the footbridge being remodelled and some general repairs undertaken at what was a very tired and dilapidated site; however, the ticket office remains, albeit now painted blue! *7 August 2008*

▶ The station once boasted a goods yard, which has long since been replaced by a small industrial estate; however, the weighbridge remains in the car park and is seen here with the site of the goods yard ahead. *7 August 2008*

Cradley Heath

Grid reference 393925/285720

Cradley Heath station opened in 1863 on the Stourbridge Railway's short line from Stourbridge to Old Hill (later incorporated into the GWR) and was originally known simply as Cradley. It is at the industrial heart of the Black Country and several branch lines ran from the main line around the station serving collieries and heavy industries. Today, however, coal-mining is a thing of the past and heavy industry has significantly declined, leaving the main line the only source of through traffic for the station.

▲ This view shows the station from the footbridge looking towards Birmingham, with Woods Lane level crossing immediately beyond the end of the platforms. When originally built, the platforms here were staggered on either side of the crossing but were later aligned as they are now following removal of the goods facilities at the station and its rebuilding. *7 August 2008*

◀ Looking south from the footbridge, DMU No 153325 stands at the Worcester platform with the site of goods facilities and sidings to both left and right of the line; the buildings partially obscured by the row of trees on the left are contemporary with the goods yard. The area to the right was reclaimed from railway use to provide a bus station and, as with many of the region's station sites, a car park. *7 August 2008*

▶ The station site is at the same level as the surrounding land so a level crossing was a necessity at Woods Lane. No 150003 enters the station with a Worcester Foregate Street via Snow Hill service. *7 August 2008*

Old Hill

Grid reference 396277/285892

Old Hill Station was opened in 1866 and is still functioning today, although it has gone through a significant change during its operational lifetime.

Located on the Stourbridge Extension of the GWR, it also served what is commonly termed the 'GWR end' of the Halesowen Railway.

▼ Looking towards Rowley Regis we see the station building and platform footbridge; the Longbridge and Dudley routes were just beyond the footbridge and were served by their own platforms and buildings. Once again I have to comment that the 'refurbishment' of the station during the last 20-30 years could have had a little more thought as the small brick building seen on the left appears out of keeping with the station and the original features of Old Hill, which can be seen in old photographs of the site and are sadly missed. *7 August 2008*

▲ The old Halesowen Railway connection would have joined
the main line to the right of this picture at the spot marked
by the metal fence and gap in the hedgerow, while the line
to Dudley via the 'Bumble Hole line' was to the left – no
observable trace remains of the platform or lines today.
7 August 2008

◀ 0-6-0PT No 7430 pauses to take on
water as it prepares to take out the
last train from the Halesowen branch
platform. The remaining part of Old
Hill station is to the right of the train.
29 August 1958; Roger Shenton

Rowley Regis

Grid reference 397957/286548

Rowley Regis station was opened in 1867 by the GWR and, uniquely on this stretch of line, has

retained its original booking office, although the rest of the site has been considerably remodelled.

▲ The station is very well maintained, and it can be seen in this view in Station Road that at some time one entrance to the building has been bricked up on the right-hand side. *15 July 2003*

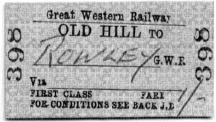

▶ At platform level the remnants of historical interest evaporate, as we see here looking towards Langley Green from the entrance pathway down from the car park; the latter area was previously occupied by a rail-connected Shell fuel terminal. *3 September 2003*

Langley Green

Grid reference 399748/288435

Langley Green station opened in 1884 under the GWR, and in 1885 was moved along the line a few hundred yards in order to serve the GWR branch line to Oldbury, which had a passenger service to its terminus between 1885 and 1916 (not to be confused with the LNWR main-line Oldbury station, now known as Sandwell & Dudley).

▲ This view of Langley Green towards Stourbridge from the Birmingham platform shows the booking office and footbridge and, in the distance, the level crossing over Station Road, beyond which was the site of the original station. *3 September 2003*

▼ This 1993 view of the station, looking in the opposite direction from the previous one, shows the large signal box on the end of the Birmingham platform controlling the junction with the former GWR Oldbury line to the left, which at that time served the nearby Albright & Wilson chemical factory and Rood End sidings (see the *Central Birmingham* volume of this series. The booking hall was also still extant on Western Road at this time, before being demolished and replaced by a platform-level ticket office during the late 1990s. *1993; Bernard Shaw*

▶ Taken from roughly the site of the signal box, we are on the Birmingham platform looking at the Oldbury branch curving away from the station under Western Road – the trackbed and platforms appear intact, albeit showing some signs of age in the case of the latter. *3 September 2003*

Oldbury Town

Grid reference 398880/289198

This station should not be confused with the LNWR's main-line Oldbury station, now known as Sandwell & Dudley. This Oldbury station formed the terminus of a short GWR branch line from the Stourbridge Junction-Snow Hill line and enjoyed a very brief operational life from 1885 to 1916. The line upon which the station stood, however, remained in use until 1995, providing rail access to Albright & Wilson's chemical works, now part of the Rhodia Group, which joined the main line at the present site of Langley Green.

▼ The area surrounding the station, due in part to its close proximity to the Birmingham Canal, was heavily developed as Oldbury Town goods, as seen here with a canal transhipment shed in the centre of the photograph. The passenger station was serviced in its later years by a half-hourly GWR 'Motor Car' service from Langley Green, taking just 3 minutes! *1910; Roger Carpenter collection*

▲ Viewed from Churchbridge, the railway and Oldbury Town station site were to the left, the station itself lying under roughly the middle of the Bingo hall. It is incredible just how quickly the signs of a railway can be erased: the ceaseless ring road/bypass building around the Black Country has accounted for the loss of many sites of railway history, and here too redevelopment has swept away most traces of the past. *21 January 2004*

▼ I spent some time walking around the area trying to find some evidence that a railway had once passed through this area. This photograph shows the remains of a railway overbridge that would have carried the branch over Seven Stars Road; Langley Green station lies half a mile or so to the right. *21 January 2004*

Route 4:
Hunnington to Dudley

The joint GWR/MR Halesowen Railway opened to traffic in 1883 in a very rural setting between Rubery, Halesowen and Old Hill. The line closed to passenger services long before it ceased operation; in 1927 it became goods only except for workers' trains to the Austin Rover works at Longbridge, which continued until 1958.

During the early 1960s, in a time of great change for the railways, research showed that almost no one used the service from Old Hill to Dudley, and even in the other direction, only during peak periods, the services were hardly working to capacity! Unfortunately these results led to the line's demise, with passenger services being withdrawn in 1964. Although the line staggered on for goods traffic for a few years, the halts were to see no use and during the late 1960s to the early 1980s virtually all trace of them was erased.

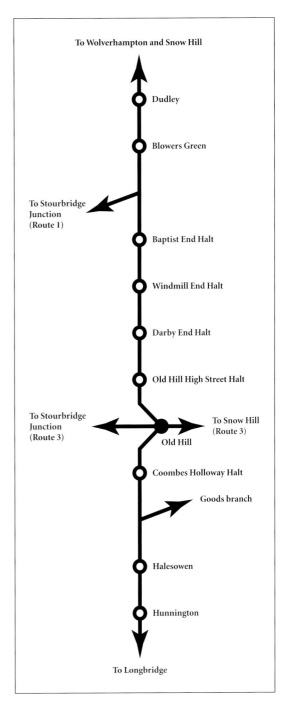

To Wolverhampton and Snow Hill

Dudley

Blowers Green

To Stourbridge Junction (Route 1)

Baptist End Halt

Windmill End Halt

Darby End Halt

Old Hill High Street Halt

To Stourbridge Junction (Route 3)

To Snow Hill (Route 3)

Old Hill

Coombes Holloway Halt

Goods branch

Halesowen

Hunnington

To Longbridge

Hunnington

Grid reference 396830/281310

Hunnington station, as with Rubery on the same line, closed to passenger traffic in 1919. However, the line remained opened to goods traffic and workers' trains to the Austin Rover works at Longbridge until 1958. The station itself also had sidings serving the nearby Blue Bird toffee factory (now closed) on the B4551 Bromsgrove Road.

▲ Here we see the grand Hunnington station building looking towards Longbridge before lifting of the track had begun; the goods siding can just be discerned to the right. In the foreground can be seen the siding breaking off from the main line for the use of the Blue Bird factory; the layout was controlled by a ground frame housed inside the hut on the left. *12 July 1953; D. J. Norton*

◀ The station house is now a well-preserved private residence. The current owners and their predecessors have done a great job in maintaining the exterior of the property: note the 'Beware of Trains' notice on the right of the building! *19 January 2007*

Halesowen

Halesowen station opened in 1878 and boasted goods yard facilities; there was also a short branch to the Halesowen Basin for the transfer of goods to and from the nearby Birmingham Canal.

▶ Looking towards Old Hill we see MR 0-6-0 Nos 58271 and 58167 with an SLS Special at Halesowen. From the early 1900s the passenger station was served by a GWR railcar service to Dudley via the 'Bumble Hole line', and there were also workmen's trains to the Austin works at Longbridge via the route through Hunnington and Rubery. *30 May 1959; Roger Shenton*

▶ This is roughly the same scene, where now a roadway for the industrial estate marks the trackbed; a small waiting room and signal box once stood where the lamppost and sign stand on the right. Just beyond the trees to the right lies Walters Somers Forge, a structure that featured in numerous period photographs of the station. Mucklow Hill is to the rear of the photographer, and once crossed the line via a bridge; however, it was considerably widened following the railway's closure and, with no need for a bridge, demolition was inevitable and Mucklow Hill is now at ground level with the trackbed. *19 November 2004*

Coombes Holloway Halt

This was the intermediate stopping point between Halesowen and Old Hill. Its existence was short, serving only from 1905 until 1927.

▶ The site of Coombes Holloway Halt at the site of the long-removed bridge that carried the line on a high embankment, much of which still exists to the rear of the photographer flanking the A459 from its junction with the A4099 towards Old Hill. *5 August 2003*

Old Hill – see Route 3, pages 47-48

Old Hill
High Street Halt

Grid reference 395947/286690

The Halt sat a short distance from Old Hill station and proved a convenient stop for the town centre a short walk away. Opening in 1905, the halt was one of four on the line, served by six trains each way daily; it saw the use of the GWR's 'Rail Motors' traversing the line until its demise in 1964.

▲ Looking towards Old Hill, the somewhat ramshackle halt is seen here in its original wooden construction shortly before the platforms and shelters were replaced with concrete structures. *16 February 1957; Michael Hale*

▼ This view shows just how much any trace of the halt has been removed. We are on Garretts Lane with Wrights Lane to our right – the halt stood on a steep embankment where the small cluster of trees now stands centre right, with the line originally crossing Garretts Lane via a bridge and running from right to left. *19 November 2004*

▼ The view from Wrights Lane shows the halt's site to the right, and the brick bridge abutment on Garretts Lane, which is still in place and is the only part of the line that has escaped redevelopment at the site. *19 November 2004*

Darby End Halt

Grid reference 395500/287618

Opening in 1905 and served by the six 'Rail Motors' in each direction between Halesowen and Dudley, Darby End succumbed to the problem of scandalously poor patronage at a time when Dr

Beeching was scouring the figures for every corner of Britain's railways with a view to major cuts. The halt closed in 1964 together with the other passenger stations and halts.

▲ GWR '6400' Class 0-6-0PT No 6418 pauses at Darby End with a single-coach Dudley to Old Hill working, having just crossed Withymoor Road bridge, the parapet of which can just be seen beyond the Dudley platform to the right. The original wooden platforms at the halt had been replaced with the concrete structures seen here several months prior to this photograph. *28 June 1958; J. Wood, courtesy of Kidderminster Railway Museum*

▶ At one of the few sites I've visited where you'd be very hard pressed to guess that a railway had ever been through it, here we are looking towards the site of the halt: the line, on an embankment, crossed Withymoor Road here via a bridge, with the halt immediately following it on the other side of the road, where the new houses stand ahead and to the left. A small piece of embankment remains and it is from the top of this (very precariously!) that this shot was taken, looking along the direction of the original track (and at roughly the right height). *19 November 2004*

Windmill End Halt

Grid reference 395695/288220

Windmill End opened in 1878, enjoyed a fairly inauspicious life and closed to passengers, with the line, in 1964. The study of passenger usage on the line that ultimately led to its demise provided an interesting fact about Windmill End: only one person a day used the halt to catch a train in the direction of Dudley!

▲ A complete refurbishment of the station has just been completed as ex-GWR '6400' Class 0-6-0PT No 6418 brings the 2.15pm Old Hill to Dudley service to a stop. As with all the halts on the line, facilities were meagre and, despite all receiving facelifts, with the coming of Dr Beeching their days were soon numbered. *28 June 1958; J. Wood, courtesy of Kidderminster Railway Museum*

▼ Due to the topography, the halt's location, as with the majority of stops on this line, is unrecognisable today. This is as close a replication as possible of the 1958 view, but the embankment upon which the line ran has been partly cut away for the building of the row of houses to the right. The only connecting features are the light-coloured houses in the centre of the shot, which are the same as those seen immediately to the right of the Pannier tank peeping above the platform in the earlier photograph. *19 November 2004*

▼ This view is taken from the remaining embankment on Springfield Road looking towards the halt site, which is roughly to the rear of the new houses to the right on Windmill End. The bridge carrying the line over Springfield Road has long since been removed. *19 November 2004*

Baptist End Halt

Grid reference 394415/288817

This was the first stop on the GWR line from Dudley to Halesowen after it left the OWWR/GWR Dudley-Stourbridge Junction line between Blowers Green and Harts Hill. Opening in 1905, with three other halts on the line, it lasted 59 years before succumbing to closure in 1964.

▲ A sorry site, this is Baptist End Halt looking towards Dudley some four years after closure with the lines lifted. In the foreground the line crosses Baptist End Road and ahead lie the two platforms that replaced the original wooden ones in 1957. *3 March 1968; Roger Shenton*

▶ With the bridge over Baptist End Road now removed, the closest it is possible to get to the 1968 perspective is seen here. As with the other 'Bumble Hole line' sites, scant evidence remains to attest to its existence. This is, of course, in part due to the change in use of much of the Black Country, with sites that were previously surrounded by coal mines, foundries and various heavy industries now being used for residential purposes. This has necessitated great changes in the landscape, with much that was observable surrounding the railway in past shots being completely obliterated, levelled, filled in or built upon. *19 November 2004*

Blowers Green – see Route 1, page 19

Dudley – see Route 1, pages 20-21

Route 5:
Sandwell & Dudley to Wolverhampton High Level and the Princes End branch

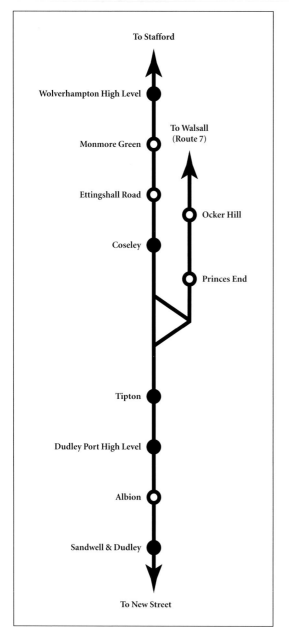

To Stafford

Wolverhampton High Level

Monmore Green

To Walsall (Route 7)

Ettingshall Road

Ocker Hill

Coseley

Princes End

Tipton

Dudley Port High Level

Albion

Sandwell & Dudley

To New Street

Continuing the journey begun in the *Central Birmingham* volume of this series along the Stour Valley line from Birmingham New Street to Wolverhampton High Level, we pick up the route at what is now Sandwell & Dudley station, formerly Oldbury & Bromford Lane, on this route heavily used by both local and cross-country services. We will also take a detour along the now lifted Princes End branch, which left the Stour Valley line at Tipton, joining the LNWR's South Staffordshire line just south of Wednesbury Town, which carried goods traffic until 1980; once closed, only a 'stub' remained between Wednesbury and Ocker Hill, which was closed in 1991.

Sandwell & Dudley

Grid reference 399300/290088

Sandwell & Dudley station opened as Oldbury & Bromford Lane on the Stour Valley Line of the Birmingham, Wolverhampton & Stour Valley Railway, opened by the LNWR in 1852 and forming a route between the newly opened Birmingham New Street and Wolverhampton High Level. During the 1960s a number of stations on this line closed, including the stations on either side of Oldbury at Spon Lane and Albion, but Oldbury

weathered the storm and in 1984 was renamed Sandwell & Dudley (initially 'Parkway' was added too). Along with the renaming came something of a change in role and status: the original wooden platform buildings were demolished and the wooden platforms removed and replaced with double-length concrete ones in order to take not only the existing local EMUs but also the main-line Inter-City trains that were now to stop here.

▲ Although the waiting rooms here are significantly more comfortable than those provided on the purely 'local' stations (indicating what the railway in general thinks of its 'bread and butter' local fare passengers), the brick used provides a rather gloomy, drab look to the whole station, as illustrated here with the Wolverhampton platform waiting room. *21 January 2004*

▶ This photo gives a good impression of the sheer length of the platforms, which does appear as a bit of a shock when visiting a 'local' station, but they were built to accommodate Inter-City main-line trains. While it is positive to see a station that has had considerable investment, as with most 'revived' stations I have a hankering for the appearance of the original wooden station with extended canopies (which were removed during the electrification programme on this line during 1966/67). *21 January 2004*

Albion

Largely overlooked by photographers during its operational years between 1853 and 1960, the Albion station site today is one of the most inaccessible in the region. Accessed from Union Street, which crossed the railway via a level crossing at the end of the platforms, the site has long since been scoured of all traces of the station, considerably aided by its largely wooden construction, with the site itself now occupied by a large industrial concern that has encompassed Union Street within its sprawling complex.

▲ Stanier 'Black Five' 4-6-0 No 45027 powers through Albion station, a year after closure, with an up working, and is about to cross the Union Street level crossing upon which the photographer was standing. The arched canopies at Albion gave the station a very distinctive appearance. *25 April 1961; Dave Williams*

◄ The site today is inaccessible, but in this view, taken from the only part of Union Street not within the industrial centre, we see the gates to the left marking the site of the level crossing, now removed. The truck to the right is standing roughly where the station building once stood. *21 January 2004*

Dudley Port High Level Grid reference 396762/291907

The 'top' station, on the Stour Valley line, opened in 1852 and was a large facility featuring numerous platform buildings for differing classes of passenger, together with a considerable station building that rose above the embankment from what is now the car park.

▲ I have to confess that on my travels I have yet to come across a more disappointing station. Especially considering the history of the railways at Dudley Port, I would have thought they could have come up with a building more appropriate than a 'Portakabin'. The original station booking office was a large two-storey 'house'-type structure. *15 July 2003*

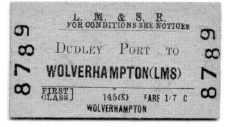

▶ Things scarcely improve at track level, as seen here looking towards Wolverhampton. The station has been reduced to a single island platform, with all the original buildings being replaced by two 'bus shelters'. The original Birmingham platform has now also completely vanished! *14 September 2008*

Tipton

Tipton station opened in 1852 as 'Tipton Owen Street' and is one of the few stations in this area that appears to have retained some of its earlier features, and indeed its operational status when considering the drastic 'rationalisation' of stations on this line and its close neighbours.

▲ The station building, seen here off Owen Street, is the original structure, with access gained through the entrance immediately under the 'Tipton' sign. There is no footbridge at the station; access between the platforms is via a subway or via the level crossing immediately off-camera to the right. *13 September 2003*

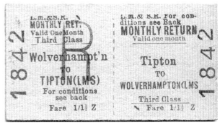

◀ This is the station building on the Wolverhampton platform, seen from the Owen Street level crossing. The platforms are of a supported wooden design and shake rather overexcitedly when trains thunder through, which they do with a high level of frequency; this has led to plans to remove the level crossing as the constant lowering of the barriers seriously hinders traffic flow along Owen Street. *13 September 2003*

Princes End

Temporarily leaving the Stour Valley line at Tipton, the first station along the Princes End branch is Princes End itself, which opened under the LNWR in 1863 and was the second station to serve Princes End; the first – on the West Midlands Railway/GWR line some mile or so away – was also named Princes End, but was later renamed Princes End & Coseley to avoid confusion. The life of the station was short, and it closed in 1890, only to re-emerge in 1895, finally closing in 1916.

▲ Nearly 100 years after closure to passengers there are still some good signs of the old line, as it continued to operate into the 1980s. The signal box controlling the Upper Church Lane level crossing looks the worse for wear shortly before its removal. *November 1981; Laurence Hogg*

▼ The line has since become a footpath running along the rear of Princes End High Street, and is seen here approaching Upper Church Lane. The signal box and crossing were ahead and to the left respectively – neither exist today. The station site stood immediately beyond the crossing. *24 October 2003*

▼ With Upper Church Lane to the rear, here we see the station site proper. The line continued from here to Ocker Hill and was retained in use for coal trains serving Ocker Hill Power Station and other goods workings until 1980. *24 October 2003*

Ocker Hill

Grid reference 397460/293927

Ocker Hill station was opened by the LNWR in 1864, only to close 26 years later in 1890. Its second incarnation didn't fare much better, opening in 1895 and closing in 1916. However, the line itself proved valuable for goods traffic, including deliveries to the then Midland

Electricity Corporation's Ocker Hill Power Station, which had opened in 1897. Unfortunately for our purposes, since the line's demise Blakeley Wood Road has emerged and been realigned; in addition, an industrial estate has been built on the area that the trackbed once occupied.

▲ In this shot, the station would have been in a cutting roughly to the right of centre behind the trees on the opposite side of the traffic island (the view is looking across to the site from Gospel Oak Road. The site is now occupied by an old people's home and a wide road off which runs an industrial estate. *24 October 2003*

◄ Off Gospel Oak Road are the remains of the filled-in cutting leading to the tunnel under the traffic island, providing the only clue as to there every having been a railway through this area. Here we can see that the cutting has been filled to ground level and is fenced off. Visible is the top of the tunnel mouth, looking roughly in the direction of the station at the junction of Gospel Oak Road with the traffic island shown earlier. Such was the unstable state of the cutting leading to the tunnel that in its latter years trains were restricted to 10mph passing through it! It was filled in when the line closed to prevent collapse and to stop underground fire holes to which it was prone. *24 October 2003*

Coseley

Grid reference 394287/294140

Back on the Stour Valley line, Deepfields & Coseley station was opened by the LNWR in 1852, only to close exactly 50 years later in 1902. Coseley station in its present setting opened in that year, 400 metres further down the track from the

original. The original station buildings, however, have long since been replaced, except for the waiting room on the Wolverhampton platform, which used to be a ticket office.

▲ Viewed here from the top of the entrance pathway to the Wolverhampton platform and looking across the station towards the small Birmingham platform waiting room, the Wolverhampton platform building can be seen to the left. *3 September 2003*

▶ From the Birmingham platform we can see that the waiting room on the Wolverhampton platform has survived the rebuilding of the rest of the station and provides the only structure of historical interest at the site today. The station itself is currently served by the half-hourly Centro service from Wolverhampton through Birmingham Snow Hill to Coventry. *3 September 2003*

Ettingshall Road

Grid reference 393175/296538

Ettingshall Road station opened in 1852 under the LNWR between what was then Deepfields & Coseley station and Wolverhampton (Monmore

Green was not opened until 1863), and closed to passengers in 1964.

▲ This photograph shows the site of the entrance to Ettingshall Road station from Parkfield Road, with little to indicate that a station once stood here. The station was of wooden construction with waiting rooms on both platforms and enjoyed only light passenger usage, succumbing to frequent tram and bus services between here and nearby Wolverhampton. *24 October 2003*

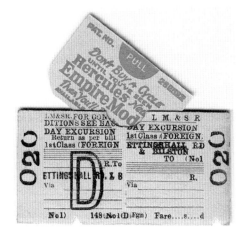

◄ A remnant of operational days: the crumbling staircase is one of the few indications of the station still surviving at the site and is in a location inaccessible to the public. *29 November 2006; Paul Baxter*

◄ Equally inaccessible is the station location site itself, seen here looking towards Wolverhampton. *29 November 2006; Paul Baxter*

Monmore Green

Grid reference 392740/297800

The station opened in 1863 on the LNWR's Stour Valley Line as the first station south of Wolverhampton. Unfortunately, it had a relatively short life and closed in 1916. Due to its extremely early closing date, I have not come across a period photograph of the site but would surmise that the station was of similar wooden construction to that at Ettingshall Road.

▶ Looking from the small area of waste ground on the corner of Bilston Road and Landport Road, a staircase leads up to the site of the station. *24 October 2003*

▶ At track level, looking towards Wolverhampton, nothing remains of the station. *21 July 2008; Paul Baxter*

▶ Looking back towards Birmingham, the bridge over Bilston Road can be seen ahead; although not discernible in this shot, the junction with a branch that served Chillington Wharf was a short distance away. *21 July 2008; Paul Baxter*

Wolverhampton High Level

Grid reference 391965/298902

Opened by the LNWR in 1852, Wolverhampton High Level station forms an important stop on the Rugby to Stafford section of the West Coast Main Line, and as such a wide variety of passenger and goods trains can be seen passing by. Unlike its Low Level neighbour, the station is flourishing – although, when you consider it in comparison with its long-demised GWR neighbour, it does make one wonder if the right decision was made!

The station entrance, viewed from Railway Drive, is hardly inspiring. In 1965 the old station was completely demolished and replaced with the present-day structures, removing all character from the site – a fate that would also befall Birmingham New Street. The rebuilding was in anticipation of the electrification of the West Coast Main Line, a move that largely rang the death knell of its former GWR counterpart. The only surviving original structure of the old station today is the Queen's building, which now functions as a café off Railway Drive. *3 September 2003*

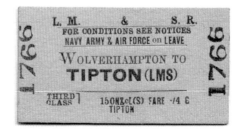

▲ We are now standing on the concourse constructed to facilitate entry to the new Platform 4 – to the left – occupying the former site of the engineer's sidings. The redevelopment of the Low Level station can also be seen above the platform canopy. I have to admit, for once, that it's nice to see some investment going into the region's railways, and any new structures could hardly diminish the aesthetics of such an uninspiring station as this. In fact, in my humble opinion, the new structure adds some visual appeal/interest to the site! *7 September 2006*

▼ Looking south towards Birmingham, Wolverhampton signal box lies immediately to the left, while ahead to the right a former goods warehouse that once served the station is the sole survivor of a series of warehouses and goods sheds. A local service is about to depart for Birmingham New Street. *3 September 2003*

Route 6:
Swan Village to Wolverhampton Low Level and Dudley

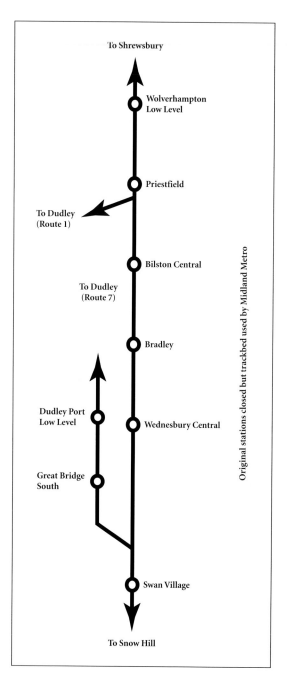

To Shrewsbury

Wolverhampton Low Level

Priestfield

To Dudley (Route 1)

Bilston Central

To Dudley (Route 7)

Bradley

Dudley Port Low Level

Wednesbury Central

Great Bridge South

Swan Village

To Snow Hill

Original stations closed but trackbed used by Midland Metro

In direct competition to the LNWR's line explored in Route 5, the GWR's connection between Birmingham and Wolverhampton opened on 14 November 1854 as a 'mixed gauge' (broad and standard) route between Snow Hill and Wolverhampton Low Level. The opening date was some two months later than planned due to the collapse of one of the bridges in Winson Green and Brunel's subsequent order for the strengthening of several other bridges on the line. While exploring this route we also take a brief diversion along the GWR's link line to the South Staffordshire line at Dudley Port Low Level, which opened in 1866.

Swan Village

Grid reference 399420/292245

Swan Village opened with the line in 1854. In 1866 the station was expanded to serve two lines with the addition of branch through Great Bridge allowing access to the lines to Dudley. Services to

Dudley ceased in 1964, and the station closed completely in 1972 together with the Low Level-Snow Hill line.

▲ Viewed from Bilhay Lane bridge, 'Hall' Class No 4092 *Aldenham Hall* builds up steam to lead a double-headed service between Wolverhampton and Snow Hill out of Swan Village. In the distance can be seen the signal box at the level crossing on Swan Lane and the original wooden station buildings, which were replaced in 1959 with brick structures. *1957; Roger Carpenter collection*

▶ The view from Bilhay Lane today shows that the station has been completely removed from the landscape together with, to the left, the Dudley line, although the curved sweep of its route is marked by the road through the industrial estate. Since 1999, some 27 years after lifting, rails are once again in situ, but this time for the light rail Midland Metro Birmingham Snow Hill to Wolverhampton St George's service. *21 January 2004*

◀ Marking the site of the station at Swan Lane level crossing, a new office building stands on the site of the Wolverhampton platform. The signal box stood immediately ahead of this point but was not required for the Midland Metro. Unfortunately the Metro didn't involve the reopening of Swan Village station but merely the complete clearance of the site, while the Black Lake Metro stop was constructed a few yards to the rear of the photographer. *21 January 2004*

Great Bridge South

Grid reference 397645/292578

Leaving the GWR main line at Swan Village towards Dudley Port, we come to Great Bridge South, which was opened by the GWR in 1866 and, apart from closure during the Great War between 1916 and 1920, remained in use until 1964. Interestingly, this station and its LNWR counterpart, which was virtually 'over the road', were both known as Great Bridge station until 1950. The locations of both are a little hard to pin down these days, as the area has been heavily redeveloped and roads realigned – including the construction of the A41.

▼ The station is seen here derelict and awaiting demolition, its wooden structure falling apart but the line still in situ. The station was at a raised level where the line crossed New Road via a bridge – however, none of this remains today. *13 December 1967; David Bathurst*

▲ This is the freshly cleared site of Great Bridge South station as viewed from New Road – the site is at the corner of New Road and Horseley Heath and, as can be seen, has been levelled. The Horseley Heath side now hosts a car showroom and some industrial units, while the New Road side is still bordered by an old railway wall. *5 December 2003*

▼ At the corner of New Road and Horseley Heath, the top of the bushes in the centre of the shot marks the level of the old station site. Some blue-brick walling can just be made out at the top of the embankment behind the car showroom, which is just out of shot around the corner on Horseley Heath. *5 December 2003*

Dudley Port Low Level   Grid reference 396752/291920

Dudley Port Low Level station opened in 1850 on the South Staffordshire Railway (later LNWR). It was known colloquially as the 'bottom' station, as the LNWR's Stour Valley line of 1852 crossed the line to Dudley and a station was opened there at the higher level. Low Level closed in 1964 together with the line upon which it stood.

▲ Viewed from the footbridge entrance to the High Level station from Park Lane East, a Stanier 'Mogul' brings a Dudley Zoo excursion train into Low Level station as a throng of eager passengers wait to embark. *c1960; Michael Whitehouse collection*

◄ The site is still recognisable, the bridge ahead providing a reference point, although today it is heavily overgrown. The trackbed has been effectively mothballed until such time as proposed extensions to the Midland Metro are made (if ever). *15 July 2003*

Dudley – see Route 1, pages 20-21

Wednesbury Central   Grid reference 398245/294615

Returning to the main line, Wednesbury Central opened in 1854 as 'Wednesbury' on the route planned by the Birmingham, Wolverhampton & Dudley Railway (under close scrutiny from the GWR) from Hockley to Bilston. As elsewhere in the region, there were two stations called

Wednesbury until 1950, when 'Central' was added to this one and 'Town' to the former LNWR facility a few hundred yards away. The station fared reasonably well, outlasting many others in the area until finally succumbing to closure in 1972.

▲ Exuding a general air of abandonment, Wednesbury Central's rather austere architecture is virtually a carbon copy of the station at West Bromwich – originality was obviously not the driving force behind the BWDR! The station was of significant size, however, and had its own goods yard and shed situated out of shot ahead to the right. *13 December 1967; David Bathurst*

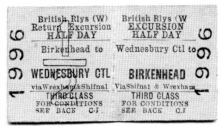

▶ Not quite as impressive a sight, the Midland Metro Wednesbury Great Western Street stop now occupies part of the site, the entrance to which can be seen to the right at the end of the Birmingham platform, with the site of the old station building in the right foreground. Not apparent in this photograph, but behind the Metro stop shelter on the Birmingham platform, and running along behind the hedgerow, is a wall dating from the old station, which appears to be the only visible remnant of the station. *10 June 2004*

◀ Unfortunately – or fortunately, depending on your standpoint – the original Wednesbury Central station has been completely obliterated (all bar the section of low walling), and the site now hosts the omnipresent industrial unit, Wednesbury Great Western Street Metro stop and, on the site of the former goods yard/shed, the Midland Metro Wednesbury Depot, seen here on the right from Great Western Street. The old station building would have been to the left with the building. *10 June 2004*

Bradley

Grid reference 396297/295255

Bradley station opened as Bradley & Moxley in 1862 and enjoyed a relatively short life, its 1915 demise flying in the face of the *Wolverhampton Chronicle*'s initial excitement at its opening: 'It will prove a great convenience to the inhabitants of the two localities named,' it announced!

◀ Looking down from Bradley Lane, there is nothing immediately recognisable as railway history at the spot where the old station once stood. However, behind the photographer is the Bradley Lane Metro Stop, a service that has breathed new life into a long-forgotten route. *24 October 2003*

◀ Midland Metro T69 tramcar 04 passes the site of the old Bradley station as it is about to pass under the Bradley Lane bridge and pull into the Bradley Lane Metro stop on its way to Wolverhampton St George's. *24 October 2003*

Bilston Central

Bilston Central was a large station, built in the same architectural style as the other BWDR-planned stations on the route, and was the second station to serve the people of the town, the other being the OWWR's Bilston West, which opened the same year. Bilston Central fared better than its counterpart by ten years, however, closing with the line in 1972.

▶ Here we see the station in 1969, serving only a skeleton shuttle service between Birmingham Snow Hill and Wolverhampton Low Level and rapidly turning into an unkempt halt. The station building, which stood on the Birmingham platform adjacent to the footbridge, has already been demolished. To dispel a common myth, Bilston Central Metro stop is not built on the site of the old Bilston Central station; the Metro stop is now sited just through the bridge in the distance, which carries what is now Hall Drive. *1969; Roger Shenton*

▶ The Black Country Route dual carriageway now crosses the line, immediately in front of the Hall Drive bridge in the first view. We are looking north from the site of the Birmingham platform. *24 October 2003*

▶ Looking in the opposite direction from the previous photographs, nothing remains at the site today to indicate that a station had once stood here. It appears that the area was cleared several years ago but no one quite knew what to do with it, so the access road was just blocked off and left to grow over. *24 October 2003*

Priestfield – see Route 1, pages 26-27

Wolverhampton Low Level – see Route 1, pages 28-29

Route 7:
Dudley to Lichfield City and the Darlaston Loop

To Burton-on-Trent

Lichfield City

Hammerwich

To Sutton Coldfield (Route 8)

Brownhills

To Cannock

Pelsall

Rushall

To Wednesfield (Route 10)

To Sutton Park (Route 10)

Walsall

Pleck

To Willenhall (Route 9)

To Aston and New Street (Route 9)

Wednesbury Town

Darlaston

To Wolverhampton Low Level (Route 6)

Great Bridge North

To Snow Hill (Route 6)

To Princes End branch (Route 5)

Dudley Port Low Level

Dudley

To Stourbridge Junction

Another of the region's long-gone routes was that connecting the South Staffordshire Railway (later LNWR) at Dudley and Walsall, via Wednesbury, which opened in 1850. We will also extend our journey via the SSR's Walsall to Lichfield City line, which opened in 1849, taking in two link lines – the Darlaston Loop and Pleck extension – the latter linking the LNWR's line with the ex-GJR Wigan to Birmingham route, opened in 1881.

Dudley – see Route 1, pages 20-21

Dudley Port Low Level – see Route 6, page 76

Great Bridge North

Grid reference 397653/292705

Great Bridge North opened in 1850 as just Great Bridge on the South Staffordshire Railway line between Dudley Port Low Level and Wednesbury Town; the 'North' was added in 1950.

Unfortunately, as with the South station, 44 years after closure in 1964 there is little left to indicate that a station ever stood at the site, which once boasted considerable goods facilities.

▲ Three years after closure, Great Bridge North is seen looking south towards Dudley Port Low Level, with New Road bridge ahead. *13 December 1967; David Bathurst*

▶ Looking towards New Road, it can be seen that the trackbed has been 'mothballed' for a proposed extension of the Midland Metro system should this ever materialise. The 1967 photograph was taken by the corner of the building ahead on the left, but unfortunately it is not possible to access the precise spot for a comparative image today.
5 December 2003

◀ Standing on New Road bridge, we are looking along the overgrown trackbed towards Wednesbury at the site of the former Great Bridge North station on an unusually sunny December afternoon. Most of the station facilities and buildings stood to the left of the tracks. *5 December 2003*

Wednesbury Town
Grid reference 398630/294535

From my perspective, this was a fascinating site to visit as it is replete with remnants of the original railway. Built by the SSR in 1850, Wednesbury Town station was at one time the junction with the branch serving the Darlaston Loop.

▼ Unfortunately, the station originally known as Wednesbury ('Town' being added in 1950) was closed in 1964, leaving the town to be served only by its GWR counterpart a few hundred yards away. Here we see the Town station in the early 1960s facing Dudley as 8F No 48724 comes off the Darlaston Loop working light-engine to Walsall. *Roger Carpenter collection*

▲ Looking from roughly the same spot but at a slightly different angle, we see that the Dudley-Walsall tracks are still in situ; however, the Darlaston branch, which branched away to the right, is no longer in evidence. The rather arboreal nature of the line here, in its 'mothballed' status in anticipation of the much vaunted and frequently delayed Midland Metro Line 2, makes the extension increasingly hard to envisage. *10 June 2004*

▼ The entrance to the station site from Dudley was via Potters Lane level crossing.. The area to the left of the track, where once the station buildings stood and through which the Darlaston Loop ran, is now occupied by a Biffa depot, which can just be made out to the extreme left, although some of the rubbish seen here appears to have missed the site! *10 June 2004*

Darlaston

Grid reference 397817/296482

Leaving the South Staffordshire main line temporarily, we visit the Darlaston Loop, opened in 1863 to connect the SSR with the GJR at James Bridge. There was one passenger station, at Darlaston, but it failed to reap significant passenger numbers and was closed by the LNWR in 1887. The name, however, lived on at the LNWR's James Bridge station, which changed its name to Darlaston in 1913, following many years of name changes to various combinations of the two names. Unfortunately, nothing now remains of the station and the trackbed at this point is now a walkway.

▲ This is the site of the station on Darlaston Road, the trackbed running under the road with the station immediately beyond the bridge. The line here was originally single-track but was doubled in 1872 with a growth in goods traffic. *10 June 2004*

◄ We have now crossed Darlaston Road, descended the pathway leading to the trackbed and are standing on the site of the Walsall platform. The line was finally closed as a victim of the Beeching 'Axe'. *10 June 2004*

Pleck

Grid reference 400000/297055

Our second detour from the SSR main line takes in the Pleck extension, which allowed the SSR to run traffic from Walsall to the GJR and on to Wolverhampton; an extension to allow traffic to run to Bescot was also constructed but wasn't provided with a passenger station. Pleck station opened in 1881 as the sole station on the line and closed in 1917, only to reopen in 1924 and close finally in 1958.

▲ Ivatt 2-6-2 No 41225 prepares to propel a Walsall passenger working out of Pleck station and under the booking office, which sat on a plinth above the rails, parallel to Bescot Road. *13 August 1958; Roger Shenton*

▼ A similar recent perspective shows that nothing remains of the station at track level, although the girder that supported the station building and its red-brick supporting pillars can still be discerned on either side of the bridge mouth. *30 October 2006; Paul Baxter*

▼ The view of the Pleck station site from Bescot Road bridge shows the clearance work that has taken place at the site over the last 50 years, although, again, the supporting girder for the booking hall can be seen at the bottom of the photograph and further remnants can be seen, including a stairwell, upon rummaging through the thick undergrowth. *10 June 2004*

Walsall

Grid reference 401118/298523

Opened in 1847 by the South Staffordshire Railway, with the coming of the line to Wichnor Junction, beyond Lichfield, in 1849 the station was considerably expanded, a process that developed further with the arrival of the Cannock line in 1859 and the LNWR's remodelling of the site in 1861, continuing until 1923 when the booking hall was rebuilt following fire damage. Unfortunately, while developing into a considerable railway hub for the region – including significant goods facilities – the Beeching Report all but closed Walsall, leaving only the service to Birmingham in operation, and it was rumoured that this too was to be removed in original drafts of the report! In the 1990s, however, things took a turn for the better at the station with the re-opening of the route through to Hednesford and later services to Shrewsbury, together with a revamp of the station in 1995.

FLOOD AT WALSALL STATION MAY 13TH 1886

▲ In this classic LNWR postcard of Walsall from 1886 the perennial curse of the station is captured – flooding. The deluge here is so extreme that a boat is the only form of transport in use at the station! *Author's collection*

◀ More than 80 years later the flooding problem had still to be addressed, as seen here as a hopeful commuter waits for news of service cancellations. *9 May 1969; David Bathurst*

▶ In 1978 the station underwent a rebuild with the construction of the Saddlers Centre and the main entrance to the station was switched to one through the shopping mall. The flooding problem had also largely been eradicated. Here we see the entrance from Station Street. *25 August 2003; Paul Walker*

▼ Unfortunately, despite continuous rebuilding, the now uninspiring view from Platform 1 looking north shows that that no period character has been retained. *25 August 2003; Paul Walker*

Rushall

One of the Black Country's forgotten stations, Rushall opened in 1849 on the newly completed South Staffordshire Railway's Walsall to Lichfield route. Unlike the rest of the stations on the line, which managed to survive until the Beeching

'Axe', Rushall succumbed to closure in 1909. Interestingly, some recent housing developments close to the site off Station Road are named Stanier Close and Ivatt Close in honour of the railway.

▲ Due to the realignment of Harden Road/Station Road and the paucity of photographic evidence available, it is nigh on impossible to pinpoint the exact location of the station here. However, early OS coordinates do appear to place it immediately beyond the crossing seen here in 1984, which survived for some 75 years after the station was demolished before final lifting of the line. *1984; Ray Durrant*

◄ With the site of the crossing immediately to the rear, today nothing remains of either the crossing or the line, the trackbed of which can be seen here heading off towards Lichfield. Connections with the earlier shot are the pitched roofing of a nearby industrial premises that can just be made out through the trees to the right and can be discerned in the distance in the 1984 photograph. *20 January 2005*

Pelsall

Grid reference 402548/303125

A victim of the Beeching attempt to remove all rail connections to Walsall, Pelsall opened on the South Staffordshire line from Walsall to Lichfield (forming part of the route from Wolverhampton to Burton-on-Trent) in 1849. It closed, together with all stations on the line, in 1965, then the line closed to all through traffic in 1983.

▲ Now forming part of a walkway between Walsall and Brownhills, this is the station two years after closure looking towards Lichfield City. *28 May 1967; David Bathurst*

▼ This recent view of the station site, with the large station booking hall ahead on the left, yields nothing of its railway past. While it is interesting that the site is still accessible, unfortunately nothing remains to evoke memories of the past. The clearance job has been rather total – at least the platforms might have been left, as on the Wombourne line or West Bromwich pre-Metro. *20 January 2005*

► I nearly crashed the car when I saw this sign, 22 years after closure of the line, at the junction of Station Road and Norton Road! *28 January 2007*

Brownhills

Grid reference 404475/305695

One of two Brownhills stations, this one opened on the South Staffordshire Railway line in 1849 and some years later came under LNWR ownership. While its Midland Railway namesake a short distance away enjoyed a relatively short life, this station remained open to passengers until the vast culling of the region's railways in 1965, under which the whole of the line from Lichfield to Walsall was closed to passengers and retained merely as a through route until 1983.

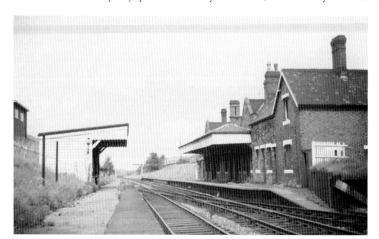

◀ Here we see the station in the early 1960s from beneath the Chester Road North/High Street bridge looking in the direction of Lichfield. Today, the site has undergone something of a major cleansing with the railway buildings being swept away and a more arboreal appearance developing at track level. *David Bathurst*

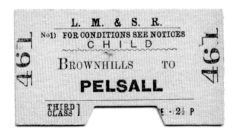

carried a lot of surface water, in and around piles of dumped refuse, which, added to the heavy foliage developing over the years, rendered a track-level exploration futile. *20 January 2005*

▼ This view is taken from what is now the A452 traffic island, looking along the trackbed towards Walsall. I wasn't completely certain of the original position of the bridge under which the 1960s photograph was taken, as considerable road realigning and building has taken place. However, after crossing to the other side of the island and looking back towards the station site, my fears of missing the correct spot were allayed when I glimpsed the blue-brick archway of the original road bridge under the 1996 concrete traffic island. *20 January 2005*

▼ If the previous photograph was the 'before', this view is the 'after' – exactly the same spot today, and totally unrecognisable. To make matters worse, the trackbed

Hammerwich

Grid reference 407365/307228

Hammerwich is one of the few sites of long-gone stations that I have visited where I have been pleasantly surprised by what remains. Opening in 1849 under the South Staffordshire Railway (later to come under the auspices of the LNWR), the station served what was then, as it is now, a relatively small semi-rural village near the Cannock coalfields. Although relatively light on passenger numbers, the station remained open to serve the Wolverhampton-Burton route until 1965 when, following the Beeching Report's complete decimation of all passenger routes to and from Walsall (apart from the New Street-Walsall service that, following a struggle, survived), the death knell was finally rung for the line as a passenger carrier.

▲ With a year to go, here we see the station looking towards Burton-on-Trent, with the station building and signal box ahead through the distinctive footbridge, the left-hand end of which leads to a public footpath through adjoining fields. The size of the station buildings, especially on the Burton platform, seem somewhat at odds with its relatively rural and remote location. *4 April 1964; Roger Shenton*

▶ A similar perspective today, taken from the footbridge, which still survives, shows that the station house has also survived as a private dwelling, although the platforms themselves have long since been removed, with a mound marking the Burton platform site. *20 January 2005*

◀ This view at Hammerwich, taken from the Burton looking towards Wolverhampton, shows the distinctive footbridge still in situ. The most notable distinction here from the 1964 photograph is the absence of the footbridge steps down to the platforms. Once redundant, the platform sections were cut off and the 'landings' blanked. *20 January 2005*

Lichfield City

Grid reference 411937/309218

Lichfield City station opened in 1849 on what was then the SSR's line, which came down through Lichfield Trent Valley and, just to the south of Lichfield City, curved west heading for Walsall. In 1884 the LNWR's Sutton Coldfield to Lichfield line was completed, forming a junction just to the south of City station.

▼ Lichfield City has retained considerable character, as can be seen in this view of the original station building on Birmingham Road, although it doesn't take much observation to see that there have been considerable changes over the years. *26 August 2003*

▶ Now consisting of an island platform with a single line on either side, the station has been considerable 'rationalised' over the years. However, the original island platform building waiting rooms are still in situ, as seen here on the Birmingham side looking towards Shenstone. *26 August 2003*

▼ The 'Engineers Siding', with a warning that electric trains should not attempt to enter, is seen here as we look towards Lichfield Trent Valley. To the far right of the picture is the area once occupied by goods sidings, now home to a skip-hire company. Despite this change of use, the weighbridge at the road entrance to the former goods yard was still in place. *26 August 2003*

Route 8:
Wylde Green to
Lichfield Trent Valley

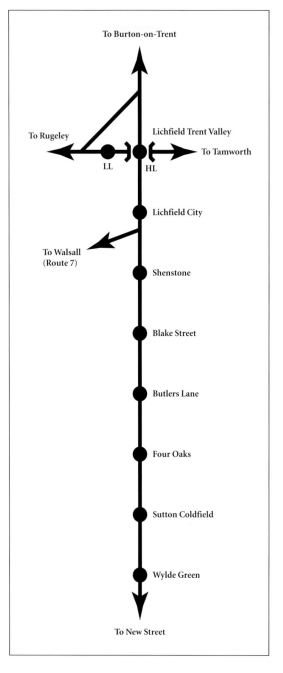

To Burton-on-Trent

To Rugeley

Lichfield Trent Valley

To Tamworth

LL   HL

Lichfield City

To Walsall
(Route 7)

Shenstone

Blake Street

Butlers Lane

Four Oaks

Sutton Coldfield

Wylde Green

To New Street

In a mood of great optimism and expansion, in 1862 the LNWR opened a line extending its route from Birmingham to Sutton Coldfield northwards to Lichfield, which provided convenient links with the SSR's route from Lichfield Trent Valley to Walsall and thus into the Black Country, together with a line north of Trent Valley through Tamworth and on to Burton-on-Trent. With hindsight, this proved to be a shrewd decision by the LNWR as the line and all of its stations have been in use ever since, enjoying a considerable investment in 1978 when they formed the northern part of the busy commuter Cross City Line, currently operated by London Midland.

Wylde Green

Grid reference 411548/294220

Opening with the line in 1862, Wylde Green station has undergone considerable restructuring with both the unveiling of the Cross City Line project in 1978 and the electrification process in the early 1990s. None of the original station buildings remain but the station is still operational and enjoys heavy peak-period passenger usage by Birmingham-bound commuters.

▲ As with a number of Cross City Line stations rebuilt in the 1970s, the station building at road level on Station Road beside the Birmingham platform is of an odd triangular-roof design. *26 August 2003*

▶ The view along the Birmingham platform looking towards the Highbridge Road overbridge and Sutton Coldfield yields little of historical interest at the site. Platform facilities are sadly meagre here with only a corrugated metal canopy protecting commuters from the elements. *26 August 2003*

Sutton Coldfield

Grid reference 411990/296382

The only survivor of three stations that once served the centre of Sutton Coldfield, this station was opened by the LNWR in 1862. The station building retains some character; its interior is heavily wood-panelling and painted in a colour scheme of navy blue and white, which gives it a somewhat unique feel on the Centro-maintained Cross City Line. Fortunately, it survived the penchant of the 1970s and 1980s of sweeping away traditional station buildings in favour of odd-shaped box-like structures (as at Kings Norton and Northfield, for example, on the southern part of the line), and, apart from the loss of some buildings and the goods sidings – which are now a car park – retains many original features.

◄ The main entrance and station building on Railway Road provide access to the Lichfield platform and, via an enclosed footbridge, the far-side Birmingham platform. The goods yard was immediately behind this building but, as with elsewhere, is no longer in existence. *26 August 2003*

◄ This view is looking back towards the station building and the entrance to the tunnel that takes the line under the centre of Sutton Coldfield; the goods sidings were to the left. The Lichfield platform once boasted a canopy matching that on the Birmingham side, but on 23 January 1955 a speeding train emerged from the tunnel, derailed and mounted the platform, resulting in the loss of 17 lives and stripping the canopy from the platform. *26 August 2003*

◄ Looking along the Lichfield platform, the lines curve away towards Wylde Green station. *26 August 2003*

Four Oaks

Grid reference 411755/297990

As with Shenstone, further along the line, and Sutton Coldfield, Four Oaks is a good example of a station that largely escaped the bland rebuilds that swept the Cross City Line from the mid-1970s onwards. Opened on 15 December 1884, the former LNWR (later LMS) station has, bar electrification, retained a traditional appearance. It also served as the temporary terminus of the Cross City Line for some time when it was reopened for local trains during the late 1970s.

▲ In this view from the station footbridge above the Lichfield lines, looking north, the station building has a comfortable waiting room – something of a rarity these days – but as is apparent that the station has been 'rationalised' over the years with largely only the island platform retaining its building. *26 August 2003*

▶ The island platform serves the Birmingham line to the left, while Lichfield is served by Platform 1 to the far right over the footbridge. *26 August 2003*

Butlers Lane

Grid reference 411063/299425

Opened by British Railways in 1957 for the introduction of DMU services between Birmingham and Lichfield – itself a sign of growing commuter usage of the line – Butlers

Lane began life as an unstaffed request stop and remained so until 1991, during the electrification of the line, when work began to construct a station building, which was completed in 1992.

▼ Here we are looking down from Butlers Lane towards Lichfield. It is interesting to note the construction differences between this station and those of the pre-BR era: Butlers Lane's platforms appear to be no more than slabs of concrete on breeze-block supports, a far cry from the craftsmanship that went into creating Sutton Coldfield or Four Oaks, for example. *26 August 2003*

▼ It must be said that, although the station has a ramped entrance as a cursory nod to disabled access, the gradient to the platforms is so steep that it is one of the less accessible stations on the Cross City Line, not to mention the fact that, with the station building on the platform itself, to obtain a ticket for a Lichfield-bound train would be somewhat of a mission. *26 May 2003*

Blake Street

Grid reference 410615/300802

Opening in 1854, Blake Street sits on what is now the county border between West Midlands and

Staffordshire. While there has been a station on this site since the 19th century, the current building is a creation of the late 20th century, a result of the investment in electrification of the route during the early 1990s.

◄ In this view, looking towards Butlers Lane, the northbound platform facilities are sadly lacking, with only a 'bus shelter' for passenger comfort. *26 August 2003*

▶ Looking across the track to the Birmingham platform, the fairly respectable waiting room to the right is a considerable improvement on the Lichfield platform's facilities. To the left is the top of the stairwell leading down to the station building and tunnel. This would suggest that the vast majority of passengers that board here are heading south! *26 August 2003*

Shenstone

Grid reference 410578/304633

The station was opened in 1884 by the LNWR and appears to retain considerable traditional character. Unfortunately, on closer inspection the 'station' element now consists of a gate at the side of the impressive building, the station now operating as an unstaffed halt. Its goods facilities, as is to be expected, are also no longer extant.

▼ The imposing station building lies on Admiral Parker Drive – however, the actual entrance to the station is by a small gate just out of sight to the left of the picture! *26 August 2003*

◀ The Lichfield platform at Shenstone, as with several others on this line, is only served by a 'bus shelter', as seen here looking north, the original structures having sadly long since been removed. *26 August 2003*

Lichfield City – see Route 7, pages 92-93

Lichfield Trent Valley

Grid reference 413645/309937

Lichfield Trent Valley is in effect two stations: the Low Level station was opened in 1847 by the LNWR on its Trent Valley line (having absorbed the creator of the scheme, the Trent Valley Railway, the previous year). The High Level line was opened by the South Staffordshire Railway in 1849, also later coming under the auspices of the LNWR. In 1871 both stations were replaced by new ones in slightly different positions. Both lines were successful and enjoyed flourishing goods and passenger traffic. High Level served the

Birmingham to Burton-on-Trent route, while Low Level served the busy West Coast Main Line. However, High Level succumbed to closure in 1965 when services to Burton via Sutton Coldfield were withdrawn, and stayed closed until the extension of the Cross City line in 1988 saw it reopen as a much reduced single-platform facility (originally the Cross City Line had operated only between Longbridge and Four Oaks, to keep within the then West Midlands Passenger Transport Executive's region and funding).

◀ A severe fire at the High Level station significantly reduced the structures at the site since, apart from the platform building itself, the canopies and assorted waiting rooms were of wood. This view on High Level Platform 3, facing Burton-on-Trent, shows that not much remains today of the original Birmingham platform. Just out of shot ahead lies Trent Valley Junction signal box, controlling the line down to the Low Level station, which is now a very seldom-used single track (originally double). *20 January 2005*

▲ Although still open, the once grand Low Level station buildings are no more and in their place some 'temporary' 'Portakabins' have been erected; however, these have been in situ for many years as the booking office, so their permanent status is unfortunately confirmed. A rather novel board erected in 1987 tells us that Edinburgh is 266 miles and London is 116 miles from here! *20 January 2005*

▶ One of the few points of interest at Low Level was Lichfield Trent Valley No 1 signal box. A splendid structure and in excellent condition when photographed, it was sadly decommissioned and demolished in early 2008. *20 January 2005*

Route 9:
Tame Bridge Parkway to Wednesfield Heath

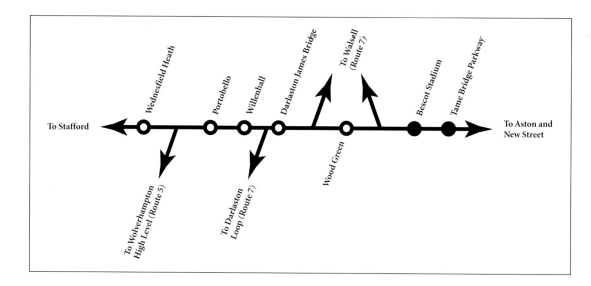

To Stafford — Wednesfield Heath — Portobello — Willenhall — Darlaston James Bridge — Wood Green — To Walsall (Route 7) — Bescot Stadium — Tame Bridge Parkway — To Aston and New Street

To Wolverhampton High Level (Route 5)

To Darlaston Loop (Route 7)

As mentioned in the Introduction, the first main line to tap into the resources of the Black Country was the Grand Junction Railway in 1837, which skirted around Wolverhampton and Walsall, although it promoted itself as serving both Walsall and Wolverhampton with stations some distance away! We join the line at one of only two passenger stations operational on the route today.

Tame Bridge Parkway   Grid reference 401770/295130

Tame Bridge Parkway station is a newcomer to the region's railway scene, having opened in 1990. It is located at the far end of Bescot yard from Bescot Stadium station on the line to Birmingham. As with the majority of newly built stations, with the exception of Smethwick Galton Bridge, it is purely functional in design and holds little interest for anyone who has an appreciation for station architecture.

◄ The station building is seen here from the car park, with the A4031 Walsall Road crossing behind it from left to right; the overhead catenary for the line can also be discerned to the left of the building. *10 June 2004*

▲ 'Jubilee' Class 4-6-0 No 45593 *Kolhapur* (now preserved) heads away from Bescot with a southbound freight under Walsall Road bridge, past what is now the site of Tame Bridge Parkway station. *28 June 1961; Dave Williams*

▼ Looking towards Birmingham from the remodelled Walsall Road bridge we see the station with Bustleholme Lane bridge in the distance. There is a 'bus shelter' on each platform and disabled access to both, one of the few good innovations in contemporary design, via ramps at both sides of the station. *10 June 2004*

Bescot

Unlike the GJR, the South Staffordshire Railway saw the merits of having a station in the heart of Walsall and opened its line from Bescot to a new station at Bridgeman Place in 1847, replaced in 1849. Under the LNWR, which absorbed the SSR and GJR, extensive goods facilities were developed at Bescot from 1881 onwards, and are still in use

today. The yard was rebuilt in 1966 at a cost of £1.5 million to handle an estimated 4,000 wagons a day. The passenger station is somewhat dwarfed by its surroundings and is now known as Bescot Stadium, following the opening of the nearby Walsall Town FC ground of that name in 1990.

▲ To enter the station requires a walk under the M6, then a walkway crosses the River Tame, after which a footbridge provides access to the two platforms. This photograph was taken from the footbridge looking towards Birmingham, with the passenger station somewhat dwarfed by the yard all around it, as seen here. *10 June 2004*

◄ Looking north from the footbridge, the line on the right diverges to Walsall, and to Wolverhampton to the left, the line with which the goods yard connects at its northern end. *10 June 2004*

Wood Green

Grid reference 399790/296508

Wood Green opened in 1837 on the GJR as 'Bescot Bridge' and was promoted as a station serving Walsall, which those with geographical knowledge of the area know is a good 2½ miles away! This misrepresentation was not lost on potential passengers, who largely ignored the station with the result that it closed on 1850. In 1881 the LNWR deemed the rail network to be sufficiently extensive and rail travel significantly popular to open another station on the site, this time called Wood Green, which fared slightly better than its predecessor, closing in 1941.

▲ The line through Wood Green is seen here during the construction of the A461 traffic island, from which the forthcoming M6 would be accessed at Junction 9. *16 April 1967; David Bathurst*

▶ A Virgin Class 390 'Pendolino' thunders past the site of Wood Green station, with Junction 9 of the M6 looming in the background. *14 September 2008*

◀ The station site today yields nothing of its former incarnation due to the total resculpturing of the landscape to encompass the M6 and the trading estate that can just be discerned at the top left of the photograph. This shot was taken from the A461 traffic island looking towards Darlaston James Bridge. *14 September 2008*

Darlaston James Bridge

Grid reference 398812/297427

Originally James Bridge station, Darlaston opened in 1837 on the then Grand Junction Railway, some nine years before it joined the London & Birmingham and Manchester & Birmingham railways to form the LNWR. In 1887 the nearby

Darlaston station on the Darlaston Loop closed, and James Bridge went through several incarnations before finally becoming Darlaston in 1913 – although James Bridge lingered on in certain references! It closed on 18 January 1965.

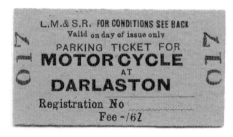

◀ The platform edge has already been cut back from the line and dereliction abounds at the station in this view looking at the Wolverhampton platform with Kendricks Road bridge ahead. *10 May 1965; David Bathurst*

▲ Kendricks Road bridge survives from the 1965 photograph, together with the factory walling – now just a façade – marking the rear of the Wolverhampton platform site. The platform is still in situ under the vegetation. *10 June 2004*

▼ We have now walked down the driveway and are looking to the station site dead ahead with the Walsall Road to our left. The area to our right, once part of the railway site, accommodated the Birmingham platform building but now serves as a children's play area in a public house beer garden. *10 June 2004*

Willenhall

Grid reference 396349/298261

Willenhall station (sometimes referred to as Willenhall Bilston Road to distinguish it from Willenhall Stafford Street a short distance away) opened in 1837 on the Grand Junction Railway's line from Warrington to Birmingham as an intermediate station between Wednesfield Heath station, loosely serving Wolverhampton, and Birmingham. However, unlike the ill-sited Wednesfield Heath, which lost its passenger services in 1873, Willenhall remained open until 1965 when passenger services ceased on the line.

▲ The station is seen looking towards Darlaston in its year of closure, with Bilston Road ahead. It is viewed from the brake-van of a goods train. Electrification of the line has already taken place and an air of dereliction looms over the station. *22 May 1965; David Bathurst*

◄ Unfortunately, a recreation of the earlier scene is not possible today, but this view, with the Bilston Road bridge ahead, is taken from roughly the spot occupied by the Birmingham platform. As can be seen, the site has been heavily scoured of station remnants, although some walling from the platform structure and associated buildings can still be found in the undergrowth to the right. Interestingly, and demonstrating the myopia of Dr Beeching et al, in 2007 plans were mooted to rebuild a station at the site if funding could be secured. *3 August 2007*

Portobello

Grid reference 395030/298633

Opening with the GJR line in 1837 to serve to mining community of Portobello, the station never ignited the interest of the travelling public and was closed in 1873 after just 36 years. The major problem appears to be that, in pre-commuter days, the majority of people worked within walking distance of their homes, so train travel wasn't a necessary part of their lives – particularly during the early years of the railway. Apart from a fatal accident on 19 October 1899, when a passenger train collided with a goods train near the station, Portobello had a relatively inauspicious history.

▼ As would be expected, some 135 years since closure the site of the station today yields nothing to indicate its past. It is seen here from Noose Lane level crossing looking towards Wolverhampton. *14 September 2008*

▼ Looking the other way from the level crossing, with the station site to the rear, we see the line heading off towards Walsall. *14 September 2008*

Wednesfield Heath

Grid reference 392805/299700

The GJR had a penchant for stations that served locations some distance away – Walsall, for example. Wednesfield Heath is another example, opening in 1837 as 'Wolverhampton' station. Not surprisingly, as with other misleadingly named stations, passenger traffic was minimal. With goods traffic always being the prime motivation behind the GJR, the station was closed to passengers in 1873 but was retained for goods use as late as 1965.

▶ The stretch of track on which the station once stood yields little today, as can be seen in this view from Station Road. The goods facilities were sited a little further along the track, but have also now been completely removed and replaced with industrial units. *11 June 2008; Laurence Hogg*

Route 10:
Sutton Town to
Wolverhampton High Level

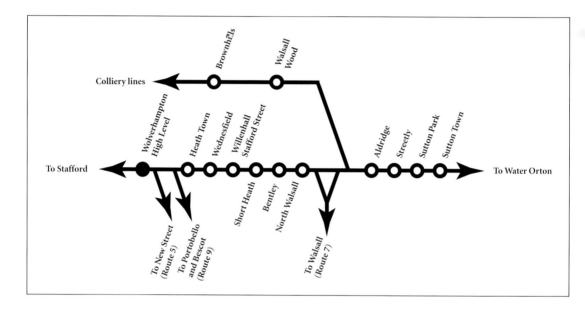

For the last journey through the region we take a trip along two now defunct routes: the Midland Railway's Walsall and Water Orton Branch and the Wolverhampton & Walsall Railway's line between those two towns. Along the way we will also take a short diversion along the ill-fated Midland Railway's Brownhills branch. Sadly, none of these routes operate passenger services today and the Wolverhampton to Walsall line has been lifted.

Sutton Town

Grid reference 412275/296412

Sutton Town station was the first passenger casualty on the Midland Railway line, which left the MR's Birmingham to Derby route between Castle Bromwich and Water Orton to reach Walsall. It then continued via the former Wolverhampton & Walsall Railway, which had been sold to the Midland Railway by the LNWR in 1876, to Wolverhampton High Level. Opening in 1879, the station closed to passengers in 1924, unlike the other stations on the line, which survived until 1965.

▲ I was very pleased to find, upon arriving at the site, that the station building on Midland Drive is completely intact and now being used as the regional headquarters for Relate – the building's nameplate shows that it is still known as the 'Station House'. *24 April 2003*

▼ The line has been retained for goods use, and it is interesting to note when pondering its demise the close proximity of this station to the LNWR's Sutton Coldfield station, still in use today, and Sutton Park station on this line, both just a few minutes' walk away – it is not surprising that passenger business was not as high as anticipated when planning the line. The building on the Water Orton platform is also still in situ but derelict and obscured from view by the row of trees on the left. *24 April 2003*

Sutton Park

Grid reference 411743/296772

This line was highly contentious as it bisected Sutton Park; being a considerably high-class area, it met with significant resistance from local landowners and residents. The Midland Railway, however, promised cheap local coal for the area, which somewhat quelled local objections, and the company went ahead and bought a 2-mile strip through the park for £6,500. The station is roughly 5 minutes' walk from the LNWR's Sutton Coldfield station and 10 minutes from Sutton Town station, and this saturation of rail cover in what was not a densely populated area contributed to the closure of Sutton Town in 1924 and withdrawal of passenger services in 1965, although the line remains open for goods traffic.

▲ No 42429 awaits clearance to move off from Sutton Park with the 5.17pm Wolverhampton-Birmingham New St passenger service. *27 July 1955; T. J. Edgington*

◄ Looking in the opposite direction, from Anchorage Road, the Birmingham platform can still be discerned to the left and the old goods shed beyond, but the station building that stood between has sadly vanished. *24 March 2004*

▲ Disappointingly, on arrival at the bottom of the entrance pathway, this is the sight that now greets visitors. This was the site of the station building, which had remained in situ until several months prior to my visit, but was demolished following frequent vandal attacks and the burning of dumped cars. The Walsall platform can be seen still in situ through the fencing to the right. *24 April 2004*

▼ We are now on Midland Road to get a shot of the goods shed, which is still standing and in seemingly good repair, and the sidings. The shed is now part of a Royal Mail sorting centre and the sidings were used for mail trains but these have now ceased. *24 April 2004*

Streetly

Streetly station opened in 1879, together with the line, and closed to passengers in 1965 when the line became goods-only. Interestingly, the station once boasted a 'Ladies Only Waiting Room'! A signal box was also located at the site.

▲ This early 20th-century view shows the station from Thornhill Road looking towards Aldridge: note the semaphore post to the right with its arm removed. *Frank Jennings collection*

◄ A comparative view today shows that nothing remains of the station site and that the area has recently been redeveloped. *24 March 2004*

Aldridge

Aldridge station opened in 1879 and was considerably expanded in 1882 with the construction of the Brownhills branch, which left the Walsall line here; it also boasted considerable goods facilities. Passenger services along the branch via Walsall Wood began in 1884 following two years as a goods-only line. The station operated until succumbing to the Beeching axe in 1965, and nothing remains at the site today to indicate that a station every stood at the spot.

▲ Taken four years after closure, we see the station still intact looking towards Wolverhampton from the mouth of the bridge that took Walsall Road over the line and from which the station was accessed. Ahead is the signal box controlling the Brownhills branch, which left the main line to the right of the box, and the considerable goods facilities here. *Dave Bathurst*

▶ Looking down to at the station site from Walsall Road, nothing remains today of the station, the Brownhills branch or the goods facilities, which stood by the cluster of new houses in the right background. The signal box stood near the distant crossover. The only remains discernible from operational days are the two pieces of brickwork nearest the camera, the right-hand of which marks the spot once occupied by a water tower. *24 March 2004*

Walsall Wood

Grid reference 404907/303510

We now move from the main line to follow the Midland Railway's Brownhills branch from Aldridge, which was a flawed attempt to turn a colliery line into a passenger route. As with Brownhills 'Watling Street' station – the only other passenger station on the branch – Walsall

Wood was opened in 1884 and closed in 1930. In 1960 the track north of the station site was lifted as the collieries began to disappear, the rest of the line to Aldridge being lifted when that station closed in 1965.

▲ Thirty-seven years after closure, the station building at Walsall Wood was still standing and in use by a builder as his yard and storage facilities. The waiting room on the opposite platform was also in situ at this time. *28 May 1967; David Bathurst*

◀ Sadly, but not surprisingly, now some 75 years after closure, nothing remains at the site to indicate a station once stood here. A children's play area now occupies the site, as seen here looking away towards Brownhills and the coalfields of Cannock. The photographer is standing on the spot where the line would have emerged from beneath Lichfield Road on its way to Aldridge or to branch off to the right half a mile or so ahead to link up with the LNWR's Leighswood line and its Lichfield-Walsall branch. A small pedestrian tunnel marks the location of the trackbed today. *21 January 2005*

Brownhills

Grid reference 403985/306183

Opening in 1884 on this most industrial of lines, the Midland Railway's Brownhills station lay a significant distance from the town centre itself, unlike its LNWR counterpart at Watling Street.

Unsurprisingly, passenger numbers were not significant and the station closed to passengers in 1930; the line continued to carry mineral trains until lifted in 1960.

▲ The station is seen here on an undated postcard, some time between 1900 and 1930, with an 'H Boiler' 3F 0-6-0 arriving with a two-coach passenger working from Aldridge. It has just crossed Watling Street bridge, the parapet of which can just be discerned beyond the station. *Roy Burrows collection, courtesy of Kidderminster Railway Museum*

▶ In this view we are approaching the station site from Watling Street, with the trackbed running parallel to this pathway to the left, and the station and booking office site ahead.
21 January 2005

◄ Not immediately discernible upon arriving at the site of Brownhill station, a rummage through the undergrowth reveals the remains of the station in these buttressed walls, all that exists today to indicate the existence of both the railway and the station. *21 January 2005*

North Walsall

Grid reference 400907/299892

Back on the main route, and moving to the Wolverhampton & Walsall Railway's section, North Walsall opened in 1872, and was subsequently incorporated into the Midland Railway in 1876. Built to serve the Walsall to Wolverhampton route via North Walsall Junction, six years after opening the station was also linked to the Midland's line from Water Orton via a stretch of line enabling the bypassing of Walsall.

▼ In 1951 the site of North Walsall doesn't yield much evidence of the former station other than the entrance pathway on the left from Bloxwich Road. Looking east, through the bridge can be seen North Walsall Junction and the box controlling it, with the Water Orton line to the left and the Walsall branch to the right. *26 May 1951; Milepost*

▲ The same site today yields even less of a clue as to its former incarnation. Due to the quagmire that the trackbed has become it was not possible to replicate the 1951 angle, so here we are looking directly down at the site with Bloxwich Road bridge to the left. *14 September 2008*

▼ Looking down from Bloxwich Lane bridge the trackbed is clearly discernible as the line heads off towards Bentley and Wolverhampton. As with the other passenger stations on the Walsall to Wolverhampton section of the line, passenger receipts were poor leading to the station closing in 1925. *14 September 2008*

Bentley

Bentley station suffered from both poor patronage and a contractual wrangle between the MR and LNWR. The latter had bought the line three years after its 1872 opening and sold it to the MR a year later, which closed the station in 1878 due to lack of passenger receipts!

▲ Some 130 years after closure, the remains of the railway as it crossed Bloxwich Lane is as close as one can get to the site of Bentley, the station being to the right up on an embankment just before the now removed bridge in an inaccessible spot now partly obliterated by the M6. The base of the bridge can be discerned here. *3 August 2007*

◀ The bridge remains on the other side of Bloxwich Lane provide a more impressive relic as we look in the direction of North Walsall station. *3 August 2007*

Short Heath

Grid reference 397425/299365

Short Heath station was opened by the Wolverhampton & Walsall Railway in 1872 off Clarke's Lane, a short distance from Willenhall Stafford Street station. Enjoying poor patronage, it was closed under LMS ownership in 1931.

▲ This is the station site following closure of the line, with the track lifted and the parapet of Clarke's Lane bridge in the foreground removed, looking towards Bentley and Walsall. *March 1969; David Bathurst*

▶ While it is not possible to completely recreate the scene today, this is the site of Clarke's Lane bridge. The platforms were situated on the embankment. *3 August 2007*

▶ At track level, between the platforms, the area has been completely sculpted as parkland – Short Heath fire station lies immediately to the left in this view looking towards Walsall. *3 August 2007*

Willenhall
Stafford Street

Grid reference 396210/298880

The Grand Junction Railway's station on Bilston Road was the first to serve Willenhall, and Stafford Street was the second, opening in 1872 as 'Willenhall Market Place'. Unfortunately, the line did not quite capture the imagination of the travelling public and services were gradually withdrawn and stations closed until the LNWR's successor, the LMS, took the decision to close the station in 1931.

▲ This view shows the abandoned passenger station looking towards Walsall, with Temple Bar bridge in the distance. The goods shed and facilities, which closed in 1965, can be seen to the right and are very much in use, while the passenger station, closed more than 25 years earlier, has retained both platforms and station building. *1957; Roger Carpenter collection*

◄ Emerging from Temple Bar bridge today shows that nothing remains of the line or the station; however, the trackbed is now a footpath through the station site, which is now part of Memorial Park with a recent development of houses now occupying the site of the former goods facilities. The station building stood immediately to our left. *3 August 2007*

Wednesfield

Grid reference 394865/299750

Opening in 1872, Wednesfield station sat in the heart of the industrial region but unfortunately the need for goods facilities and lines vastly outstripped the need for passenger services, a point not lost in the post-Grouping era by the LMS, which closed the station in 1931.

▲ There have been a few sites that have disappointed me during my travels researching this book, but few more so than this! This old photograph, looking towards Wolverhampton, inspired me to hope that there would be some remains here, but I was sorely disappointed. As the photograph shows, the site and the line continued for goods traffic way beyond the cessation of passenger services. *1960; David Wilson*

▶ At the former entrance to the station building and the site of the goods yard today can be seen this building, occupied by the NHS. The line itself passed from left to right on the other side, and following closure was lifted and replaced by Wednesfield Way. The Neachells Lane bridge from which David Wilson took his photograph has also now been removed immediately to our left. *7 September 2006*

Heath Town

Grid reference 393145/99377

Opened by the Wolverhampton & Walsall Railway in 1872, Heath Town station was just a stone's throw from the GJR's Wednesfield Heath station, and became a very early victim of the slow death of passengers services along the line, succumbing to closure under the Midland Railway in 1910.

▲ Now a crumbling relic of a lost line, I was pleasantly surprised to see the this bridge still partly in situ as I approached the site along Grove Street. The station site was to the left. *7 September 2006*

◀ As is often the case at such a site, the negotiation of a considerable amount of brambles and assorted vegetation was necessary before finding any indication of the site's former life. This buffer stop was discovered hidden in the undergrowth, looking towards Wolverhampton, while the station site itself, so far as could be made out, was roughly at this spot stretching behind the photographer. Credit must go to my son Christopher for unearthing this find as I battled the brambles! *7 September 2006*

Wolverhampton High Level – see Route 5, see pages 70-71

Chasewater Railway

The Severn Valley Railway and Chasewater Railway are the only preserved railways operating heritage diesel and steam locos on their own rails in the region covered by the *Rail Around Birmingham* series. In terms of status and publicity, the Chasewater Railway comes a distant second to the Severn Valley, but that doesn't diminish its contribution to the region's railway heritage. With a history dating back to 1959, it predates the SVR and, in the face of considerable adversity, has managed to improve and expand in recent years. The railway operates a selection of diesel and steam locos – largely of industrial origin – along its 2-mile route.

Promoted as 'The Colliery Line' – since it occupies part of a Midland Railway colliery line that skirted the site of the MR's Brownhills West station (obliterated by the construction of the M6 Toll Road), and is situated at the heart of the Cannock coalfields – the majority of the line has been built by the Chasewater Railway itself, no mean feat considering some of the engineering challenges faced by the company in undertaking such expansion.

▼ The line begins at Brownhills West station, which also accommodates the engine shed, museum and heritage centre, then follows a route around the Chasewater Reservoir, built to feed the Essington & Wyreley Canal.

▲ Another view of Brownhills West station.

▼ The passage across the reservoir, known as 'The Causeway', is a considerable feat for a railway such as the Chasewater, and one that, had it not been undertaken, would have rendered the railway defunct. It involved the laying of 120,000 tons of fill!

▶ The line crosses the reservoir at its northern tip and passes through Norton Lakeside halt in the heart of the Chasewater Country Park, where passengers can join a path through heathland designated a Site of Special Scientific Interest.

▶ The line crosses the reservoir at its northern tip and passes through Norton Lakeside halt in the heart of the Chasewater Country Park, where passengers can join a path through heathland designated a Site of Special Scientific Interest.Chasewater Heaths station, seen here on a very bleak winter's day during track-relaying on 8 January 2006, is the only staffed station on the route apart from Brownhills West, and contains a gift shop and thriving cafe.

▶ Chasetown Church Street was opened in 2004 and forms the end of the line. It consists of a single platform and run-round loop and is located near the Chasewater Nature Trail.

Index of locations

Albion 62
Aldridge 115

Baptist End Halt 59
Bentley 120
Bescot (Stadium) 2, 104
Bilston Central 79
Bilston West 25-26
Blake Street 98-99
Blowers Green 19
Bradley 78
Brettell Lane 2, 14-15
Brierley Hill 15-16
Brockmore Halt 33
Bromley Halt 34
Brownhills (MR) 117-118
Brownhills (Watling Street, LNWR) 90
Butlers Lane 98

Chasewater Railway 125-127
Compton Halt 41
Coombes Holloway Halt 55
Coseley 67
Cradley Heath 46-47

Daisy Bank 24
Darby End Halt 57
Darlaston 84
Darlaston James Bridge 106-107
Dowery Dell viaduct 8
Dudley 20-21
Dudley Port High Level 63
Dudley Port Low Level 76
Dunstall Park 30-31

Ettingshall Road 68

Four Oaks 97

Gornal Halt 36
Great Bridge North 81-82
Great Bridge South 74-75

Halesowen 55
Hammerwich 91-92
Harts Hill 18
Heath Town 124
Himley 37
Hunnington 54

Langley Green 50-51
Lichfield City 92-93
Lichfield Trent Valley 100-101
Lye 44-45

Monmore Green 69

North Walsall 118-119

Ocker Hill 66
Old Hill 47-48
Old Hill High Street Halt 56
Oldbury Town 51-52

Pelsall 89
Penn Halt 40
Pensnett Halt 35
Pleck 85
Portobello 109
Priestfield 26-27
Princes End 65
Princes End & Coseley 23

Round Oak 16-17
Rowley Regis 49
Rushall 88

Sandwell & Dudley 61
Shenstone 99-100
Short Heath 121
Stourbridge Junction 12
Stourbridge Town 13
Streetly 114
Sutton Coldfield 96
Sutton Park 112-113
Sutton Town 110-111
Swan Village 73-74

Tame Bridge Parkway 102-103
Tettenhall 42-43
Tipton (Owen Street) 64
Tipton Five Ways 22

Walsall 86-87
Walsall Wood 116
Wednesbury Central 77-78
Wednesbury Town 82-83
Wednesfield 123
Wednesfield Heath 109
Willenhall (Bilston Road) 108
Willenhall Stafford Street 122
Windmill End Halt 58
Wolverhampton High Level 70-71
Wolverhampton Low Level 8, 28-29
Wombourn 38-39
Wood Green 105-106
Wylde Green 95